Minority Enterprise
in Construction

D0844111

Robert W. Glover

The Praeger Special Studies program—utilizing the most modern and efficient book production techniques and a selective worldwide distribution network—makes available to the academic, government, and business communities significant, timely research in U.S. and international economic, social, and political development.

Minority Enterprise
in Construction

PRAEGER SPECIAL STUDIES IN U.S. ECONOMIC, SOCIAL, AND POLITICAL ISSUES

Praeger Publishers   New York   London

Library of Congress Cataloging in Publication Data

Glover, Robert W
    Minority enterprise in construction.

    (Praeger special studies in U.S. economic, social,
and political issues)
    Bibliography: p.
    1. Construction industry--United States.
2. Minority business enterprises--United States.
3. Building trades--United States.   I. Title.
HD9715.U52G55   338.6'42   77-10650
ISBN 0-275-24070-3

PRAEGER SPECIAL STUDIES
200 Park Avenue, New York, N.Y., 10017, U.S.A.

Published in the United States of America in 1977
by Praeger Publishers,
A Division of Holt, Rinehart and Winston, CBS, Inc.

789   038   987654321

ACKNOWLEDGMENTS

I would like to express my gratitude to the many people who assisted in this study.

In the academic community, useful ideas and suggestions for improvement came from Vernon Briggs, Jr., Ray Marshall, and Albert Shapero of the University of Texas at Austin and Theresa R. Shapiro of the University of New Orleans.

In the field, many persons were of great assistance. Staff personnel of several minority contractors associations provided vital help. Special thanks in this regard are due to Robert Lopez, Roy Barbosa, Herbert Williams, Ray Davis, Douglas Crosby, Phyllis Bell, Paul King, and Luis Gill. Of course, my thanks are also due to the contractors who consented to answer what must have, at times, seemed an endless stream of questions.

The Manpower Administration of the U.S. Department of Labor provided the funding that made this study possible. Much gratitude is due to Ellen Sehgal for her help during the course of the study.

Two interviewers—George Wilson of San Francisco and Kathy Ortez of Chicago—turned in outstanding performances on difficult assignments. Robert Edwards, José Flores, Luis Gregorio-Roca-solano, and David Leal helped to perform the tedious chore of coding, tabulating, and verifying the estimated 40,000 bits of information secured in the interviews. Jane Tonn, Louise Bond, Sandra Olmstead, and Kyna Simmons typed various versions of this manuscript. Sandra Illig assisted with editing.

To all, I offer my sincere appreciation while reminding the reader that I alone am responsible for any errors and omissions in the final product.

The material in this report was prepared under contract No. 81-46-70-24 from the Manpower Administration, U.S. Department of Labor, under the authority of Title I of the Manpower Development and Training Act of 1962, as amended. Researchers undertaking such projects under government sponsorship are encouraged to express freely their professional judgment. Therefore, points of view or opinions stated in this document do not necessarily represent the official position or policy of the Department of Labor. Reproduction, in whole or in part, is permitted for any purpose of the U.S. government.

CONTENTS

LIST OF TABLES

x

LIST OF ACRONYMS

AAC&TC	Atlanta Associated Contractors and Trades Council, Inc.
ABC	Associated Building Contractors
ACT	Action Construction Team (a program of the Small Business Administration)
AGC	Associated General Contractors
AIEC	Associated Independent Electrical Contractors
BAT	Bureau of Apprenticeship and Training
CCAC	Construction Contractor Assistance Center
CDC	Community Development Corporation
CETA	Comprehensive Employment and Training Act
EEOC	Equal Employment Opportunity Commission
FHA	Federal Housing Authority
GSCA	General and Specialty Contractors Association
HUD	Department of Housing and Urban Development
IBEW	International Brotherhood of Electrical Workers
LULAC	League of United Latin American Citizens
MACA	Mexican-American Contractors Association
MCAP	Minority Contractors Assistance Program
NAACP	National Association for the Advancement of Colored People
NAB-JOBS	National Alliance of Businessmen-Job Opportunities in the Business Sector
NAMC	National Association of Minority Contractors
OFCC	Office of Federal Contract Compliance (in 1975 renamed the Office of Federal Contract Compliance Programs)
OFC	Opportunity Funding Corporation
OJT	on-the-job training
OMBE	Office of Minority Business Enterprise
RTP	Recruitment and Training Program
SAC	State Apprenticeship Councils
SBA	Small Business Administration
SER	Operation Service, Employment, and Redevelopment
SFRA	San Francisco Redevelopment Agency
SMSA	Standard Metropolitan Statistical Area
UDC	Urban Development Corporation

The construction industry offers special potential to improve the economic status of minorities. It is a high-wage, growth industry with a relatively large number of blacks already in it. Many construction businesses can be formed without high capital requirements, and the easy freedom of entry makes the growth of employment and entrepreneurial opportunities for additional minorities more attainable relative to other industries.

In addition, as several writers have pointed out, government is heavily involved in the industry, making it possible for those interested in improving the economic opportunities of minorities to use their political power to influence public policy in this direction. Of the $150 billion expended on construction, approximately $30 billion, or 20 percent, is federally assisted, giving the government considerable leverage over the industry.[1]

Upgrading minority firms in construction also is appealing from the standpoint of the potential it offers to assist in integrating building-trades unions. Despite recent progress in minority participation in apprenticeship,[2] and despite the fact that more minorities work in construction than in some other industries, a lower proportion of minority construction workers are unionized than any minority workers in any industrial grouping in the United States.[3] Some view the upgrading of minority construction contractors as a strategy for either inducing the building trades to integrate (presumably by making minority firms so strong that the building trades cannot afford to ignore them) or as a way of bypassing unions altogether.

Construction work has high visibility; the contrast between white firms and white workers building in predominantly black areas while large numbers of unemployed black men stand by idle, is too obvious to miss—especially as predominantly black urban areas become sites of rebuilding activity.

Further, stimulating minority entrepreneurship in construction may generate favorable influences on minority youth. Successful minority entrepreneurs are likely to become significant role models to younger minorities, encouraging others to follow in their footsteps and thus reducing the present severe underrepresentation of minorities among company owners and managers. In fact, if the process of role modeling operates as data in this study suggest, encouraging minority entrepreneurship may have a cumulative beneficial effect: establishment of a few successful minority contractors may draw out many more.

Finally, upgrading minority contractors is likely to generate greater income and employment in the minority community. Because minority firms are more likely than other firms to hire minority workers and spend monies with minority suppliers, a larger proportion of construction funding will end up in minority hands. In addition, through a multiplier effect, initial expenditures will provide additional income and employment generation in the minority community.

Although minority capitalism cannot by itself provide employment to all unemployed and underemployed minorities,[4] it can provide some meaningful employment opportunities for them. Furthermore, there is limited evidence to suggest that for a given amount of funds, assisting minority firms in construction work offers relatively greater employment generation than does assistance to other types of minority business enterprise.[5]

METHODOLOGY

The pilot phase of this project was undertaken in two relatively nonunion southern cities—Houston and Atlanta—during the period 1970-72. Between 1972 and 1974, the study was expanded to two heavily unionized areas outside the South—Chicago and the San Francisco-Oakland area. The second-phase project sought especially to determine how minority contractors operated in a heavily unionized environment, to provide a national perspective from which to make recommendations with regard to utilizing upgraded minority construction contractors and their employees to help increase minority participation in the construction industry, and to compile data on a counterpart group of white contractors for the sake of comparison. The third objective was to test the hypothesis that the problems minority contractors face are simply problems faced by all small businesspeople—in other words, problems that arise from being small rather than from belonging to a minority.

Unfortunately, interviews with white contractors did not work out well, primarily because of the difficulties of obtaining a truly counterpart sample. Our approach was to locate the white contractor sample by asking minority contractors whom they compete against. Unfortunately, most of the smaller minority contractors were unable to specify any white contractors with whom they competed, while the few large minority competitors generally named the largest construction firms in the city. Upon verification it was generally discovered that the interviewed minorities had competed with them only rarely. Perhaps the minorities took it as a matter of pride that they competed with the biggest, or perhaps the names of the largest contractors just came to mind most readily because their trade names were most established. Whatever the reason, the approach was unsuccessful in leading us to a counterpart sample of white contractors; and this portion of the project was abandoned after initial testing in the San Francisco-Oakland area. However, the minority firms' inability to name their white counterparts was revealing in itself; and the results obtained from the survey of noncomparable whites did yield some useful information, which is detailed in the appendix tables.

SELECTION OF THE CITIES

Each of the cities studied offers an important market for minority enterprise in construction. Each city chosen has a large minority population and a significant number of minority firms in construction. Atlanta and Houston are two of the largest, most important, and fastest-growing cities in the South. One out of every ten construction jobs in the South was in these cities in 1972.[6]

The San Francisco area and Chicago are also interesting from another perspective: they are key centers of activity in the movement to upgrade minority firms in construction. The National Association of Minority Contractors (NAMC) was founded in San Francisco, and Minority Builder magazine was begun there. The earliest efforts to assist a local group of minority contractors from various trades were begun under financing from the Ford Foundation to the General and Specialty Contractors Association in Oakland. In addition, the Oakland group also had long experience in training through Project UPGRADE, a training program that served as a model for projects in Columbus, Ohio, Tacoma, Washington, and other cities around the nation.[7]

Chicago was the site of the NAMC's labor project, the first project undertaken by the NAMC under federal funding. Chicago is also the focus of operations for several minority organizations active in efforts to upgrade minority enterprise in construction.

LOCATING AND INTERVIEWING MINORITY CONTRACTORS

After the cities were selected, an interview instrument was developed and tested, and the task of identifying minority contractors was begun. The general procedure followed was to compile a master list of minority contractors from every conceivable source, including listings such as the Registry of Minority Construction Contractors and Registry of Minority Contractors and Housing Professionals, lists and referrals from Urban League chapters, business-development organizations, government agency procurement officers, material suppliers, unions, membership and mailing lists from associations of minority contractors, and construction listings in minority business directories. In addition, telephone books were examined for names of Spanish-surnamed contractors, and, in Houston, a series of announcements was broadcast on a Spanish community-affairs radio program, seeking to elicit names of contractors who might wish to be included in the survey. Finally, and most fruitfully, minority contractors interviewed made referrals to fellow minority contractors. The Polk City Directory was used to trace contractors from incomplete references.

An interview sample of contractors was selected with a view to obtaining as complete a cross-section as possible. Although large and small contractors from almost every trade were interviewed, contractors in the mechanical trades* were given special attention. Of all identified minority contractors in the four metropolitan areas, 25 percent were interviewed, including 43 percent of contractors with at least one paid employee.

The black and Spanish-heritage contractors reached were remarkably willing to be interviewed. In Houston, Chicago, and Atlanta, the non-response rate was less than 5 percent. In San Francisco, it was under 10 percent. In contrast, white and Asian-American contractors were less cooperative. Among white and Chinese-American firms, approximately one in four contractors refused to be interviewed. Many Chinese contractors appeared distrustful of any interviewer—even interviewers who spoke Cantonese. White contractors who refused interviews indicated that they were too busy.

Such a low nonresponse rate helps to assure that the sample of minority contractors interviewed—especially black and Spanish-heritage contractors—does not reflect bias owing to nonresponsive-

---

*The mechanical trades include 6 of the 17 crafts in the building trades, namely, electricians, elevator operators, ironworkers, operating engineers, pipe trades (including plumbers, steamfitters, sprinkler fitters, and pipefitters), and sheet-metal workers.

ness. Aside from white and Chinese-American contractors, nonresponsiveness reflected mainly the mood and personality of the individual interviewer.

This study relies primarily on interview data. In general, interviews with contractors covered four areas of concern: (1) background of the contractor, (2) profile of his firm, (3) problems of his firm, and (4) the contractor's view of upgrading efforts. In all, interviews with 340 active contractors, including 25 white contractors, were conducted.

To supplement the information obtained from the contractors, interviews were conducted with 300 union officials, civil rights leaders, government officials, contractors' association staff members, surety agents, and other knowledgeable persons who had pertinent information. Table 1.1 classifies all interviews conducted.

OUTLINE OF THE BOOK

Chapter 2 presents a summary profile of the contractors interviewed. Chapter 3 discusses problems faced by the minority contractors, as viewed by the contractors themselves. Both Chapters 2 and 3 rely on the data presented in the Appendix. The reader who wishes more than a summary is invited to review the tables in this Appendix, which detail the information collected in the interviews with contractors. For purposes of comparison, data in the tables are arranged by city and by ethnic or racial group. In the San Francisco-Oakland area, Spaniard-Americans (that is, from Spain) are separated from Spanish-Americans because the former were vocal in not identifying themselves as a minority group. The term "Spanish-American" covers Mexican-Americans in Houston, Chicago, and the San Francisco areas as well as Latins of Central or South American origin in the latter two cities. Japanese-Americans are separated from Chinese-Americans because the two groups are very different.

The remainder of the book is devoted to a discussion of various efforts to upgrade minority business in construction. Chapter 4 discusses approaches of demand stimulation and of supply development. Chapters 5 and 6 review two vehicles that conceptually combine demand stimulation and supply development: the minority contractor association and the joint venture. Chapter 7 contains a summary, conclusions, and recommendations.

TABLE 1.1

Schedule of Persons Interviewed

Classification	Houston	Atlanta	Chicago	San Francisco–Oakland	Elsewhere	Total
Active minority construction contractors						
Black	13	53	27	92	—	185
Spanish–American	53	—	18	33	—	104
Asian–American	—	—	—	24	—	24
American Indian	—	—	—	2	—	2
Active white construction contractors	—	—	—	25	—	25
TOTAL: ACTIVE CONTRACTORS	66	53	45	176	—	340
Other Individuals Interviewed						
Experts from the private sector: construction and related industries						
Construction industry executives (white contractors)	2	—	3	5	—	10
White contractors' association officials	4	—	1	1	1	7
Architects	1	1	—	—	—	2
Insurance industry executives	2	—	—	—	5	7
Chamber of commerce officials	2	—	—	—	—	2
Others	2	2	4	—	3	11
University experts and other consultants	4	5	—	—	7	16

Antipoverty agencies and economic development organizations					
Antipoverty agency and manpower agency officials	6	—	2	13	—	21
Model cities, urban renewal, and redevelopment agency officials	4	1	2	2	4	13
Economic development organizations	4	2	1	2	8	17
Federal government officials						
OFCC and other EEO officials	6	2	—	1	3	12
SBA and OMBE officials	3	2	2	5	4	16
HUD officials	1	4	—	1	2	8
Others	—	—	3	1	6	10
State government officials						
Employment service	2	—	—	—	—	2
Other	—	—	2	3	6	11
Local government officials	6	2	—	—	1	9
Union officials	1	2	1	1	2	7
Minority contractors' association officials and contractor assistance center officials	2	4	6	9	69	90
Civil rights organization officials	3	3	4	1	8	19
Inactive minority construction contractors						
Retired	1	3	—	—	—	4
Out of business	—	4	—	1	—	5
Planning to enter business	—	—	—	1	—	1
TOTAL: OTHER INDIVIDUALS	56	37	31	47	129	300
TOTAL: ALL PERSONS	122	90	76	223	129	640

Source: Personal interviews. Data for Atlanta and Houston were gathered in 1971. Data for Chicago and San Francisco were collected during 1973–74.

NOTES

1. William B. Gould, "The Seattle Building Trades Order: The First Comprehensive Relief against Employment Discrimination in the Construction Industry," Stanford Law Review 26 (April 1974): 775.

2. See Herbert Hammerman, "Minorities in Construction Referral Unions—Revisited," Monthly Labor Review 96 (May 1973): 44-46.

3. U.S. Bureau of Labor Statistics, Selected Earnings and Demographic Characteristics of Union Members, 1970, Report 417 (Washington, D.C.: Government Printing Office, 1972), table 13, p. 27.

4. For a controversy over the employment-generating effects of black capitalism, see Andrew Brimmer and H. S. Terrel, "The Economic Potential of Black Capitalism," Public Policy 19 (Spring 1971): 289-308.

5. See, for example, Timothy Bates, "Employment Potential of Inner City Black Enterprise," The Review of Black Political Economy 4 (Summer 1974): 64-65.

6. U.S. Bureau of Labor Statistics, Employment and Earnings in the States and Areas: 1939-1972 Bulletin (Washington, D.C.: Government Printing Office, 1973).

7. Personal interview with Gene Johnson, executive director, Project UPGRADE, Inc., Oakland, November 7, 1972.

2

PROFILE OF MINORITY CONTRACTORS AND THEIR FIRMS

Just how many minority contractors exist has long been a matter of uncertainty. Based on data collected by the Ford Foundation, one study concluded, "In 30 states comprising 107 cities for which information on Negro contractors is available, it is estimated that no more than 1,500-2,000 black contractors are in business."[1] In 1970, Joseph Debro, executive director of the NAMC, suggested a similar estimate—2,000 or .2 percent of all contractors in the nation.[2] In a 1969 survey of 48 cities, the National Association for the Advancement of Colored People (NAACP) reportedly identified 4,000 minority contractors. However, of this number, they were able to contact and interview only 2,051.[3] A study by the Small Business Administration (SBA) in 1969 placed the number at 2.6 percent of all construction firms.[4] In 1971, SBA estimates were more conservative: of the 870,000 identifiable firms in the construction industry nationwide, not more than 8,000 or .9 percent were said to be owned by minority group members.[5]

Later censuses of minority enterprise made by the Department of Commerce indicated that all previous estimates were low. A census of minority businesses in 1969, using information from income tax returns, social security card applications, and mailed questionnaires, found a national total of 29,695 minority-owned firms in contract construction, 8,214 of which had paid employees. A second census conducted in the same manner in 1972 revealed 39,875 firms, of which 9,096 had paid employees.

For the minority groups in the four metropolitan areas studied, Minority-Owned Businesses: 1972 reported a total of 3,226 firms, with 742 or 23 percent having paid employees.

Unfortunately, the census only counted minority contractors; it did not identify them. Published sources listing names of minor-

TABLE 2.1

Numbers of Reportedly Active Minority Construction Contractors, by City, Ethnic/Racial Background, and Specialty

Specialty	Atlanta, 1971 Black	Houston, 1971 Mexican-American	Houston, 1971 Black	Houston, 1971 Total	Total, Cities in South	Chicago, 1974 Black	Chicago, 1974 Spanish-American	Chicago, 1974 Total
General building contractors	45	18	28	46	91	124	12	136
Highway and street construction	—	—	1	1	1	—	—	—
Sub or specialty contractors								
Acoustical	—	—	1	1	1	—	—	—
Air conditioning, heating, refrigeration	7	10	3	13	20	28	—	28
Carpentry—framing trim, cabinets	11	21	5	26	37	44	5	49
Concrete	3	4	15	19	22	20	1	21
Dry wall	3	2	—	2	5	4	—	4
Electrical	7	3	6	9	16	60	8	68
Elevator and escalator	—	—	—	—	—	—	—	—
Excavating and grading	4	—	1	1	5	4	1	5
Floor covering (except wood)	3	4	1	5	8	7	—	7
Floor (wood)	4	—	—	—	4	2	—	2
Glass and glazing	—	1	1	2	2	5	—	5
Hauling (construction materials)	—	2	5	7	7	2	—	2
Insulation	—	—	—	—	—	—	—	—

Trade								
Ironwork—ornamental, structural, reinforcing, fencing	5	4	—	4	9	12	1	13
Landscaping	2	1	1	2	4	8	1	9
Masonry—brick, block, and stone	20	4	3	7	27	20	2	22
Painting, decorating, paperhanging	16	13	3	16	32	50	2	52
Plastering and lathing	3	1	—	1	4	18	—	18
Plumbing	9	13	25	38	47	37	4	41
Roofing (wood shingle, composition, hand-split shake)	3	6	4	10	13	10	1	11
Sheet metal	—	—	—	—	—	9	—	9
Tile and terrazzo (precast and poured)	3	40	1	41	44	8	—	8
Wrecking and demolition	1	—	—	—	1	7	—	7
Other	—	2	—	2	2	—	4	—
Trade unknown	—	—	—	—	—	13	—	17
Related trades								
Building maintenance*	3	—	2	2	5	—	—	—
TOTAL	152	149	106	255	407	492	42	534

(continued)

(Table 2.1 continued)

Specialty	San Francisco–Oakland, 1974					Total, Cities in non-South	Total Minorities, All Cities
	Black	Spanish-American	Asian-American	American Indian	Total		
General building contractors	58	24	42	1	125	261	352
Highway and street construction	—	—	—	—	—	—	1
Sub or specialty contractors							
Acoustical	—	—	—	—	—	—	1
Air conditioning, heating, refrigeration	1	2	1	—	4	32	52
Carpentry—framing trim, cabinets	3	3	9	1	16	65	102
Concrete	8	2	1	—	11	32	54
Dry wall	2	1	1	—	4	8	13
Electrical	11	5	9	—	25	93	109
Elevator and escalator	—	—	—	—	—	—	—
Excavating and grading	6	2	—	—	8	13	18
Floor covering (except wood)	7	—	1	—	8	15	23
Floor (wood)	—	1	1	—	2	4	8
Glass and glazing	1	—	—	—	1	6	8
Hauling (construction materials)	2	2	—	—	4	6	13
Insulation	—	—	—	—	—	—	—
Ironwork—ornamental, structural, reinforcing, fencing	2	—	13	—	15	28	37

Landscaping	—	11	1	—	12	21	25
Masonry—brick, block, and stone	1	—	—	—	1	23	50
Painting, decorating, paperhanging	12	8	16	—	36	88	120
Plastering and lathing	5	1	—	—	6	24	28
Plumbing	11	7	10	—	28	69	116
Roofing (wood shingle, composition, hand-split shake)	3	2	—	—	5	16	29
Sheet metal	3	2	—	—	5	14	14
Tile and terrazzo (precast and poured)	4	3	2	—	9	17	61
Wrecking and demolition	7	2	—	—	9	16	17
Other	—	—	—	—	—	—	2
Trade unknown	—	—	—	—	—	17	17
Related trades	—	—	—	—	—	—	
Building maintenance*	—	—	—	—	—	—	5
TOTAL	147	78	107	2	334	868	1,275

*Building maintenance firms were not included in the survey of Chicago and San Francisco–Oakland.

Sources: Data were compiled from membership and mailing lists of minority contractor associations, from black business directories, from referrals by suppliers, unions, and contractors, from lists of contractors generated by civil rights groups and government agencies, from a check of Spanish–surnamed listings in telephone directories, from inspections of building sites, from tours of minority neighborhoods to look for business advertisements, and (in Houston) from referrals obtained through an advertisement on a Spanish community–affairs television program.

ity contractors in the four metropolitan areas studied showed far
fewer contractors. Most of these sources defined "construction
contractor" in the broadest sense, that is, "If someone presents
himself or herself to the public as a contractor who performs construction for money, he or she is so classified."[6] Using the same
definition, the present survey uncovered names and at least sketchy
information on a total of 1,275 minority contractors in Atlanta,
Houston, Chicago, and San Francisco-Oakland. A distribution of
reportedly active minority contractors, classified by respective
construction specialty, is provided in Table 2.1.

The figures must be approached with some caution because
not all of the contractors could be reached for verification. Since
business turnover in the construction industry is high and since
some of the information utilized was as much as five years old,
undoubtedly some of those named had died, retired, moved, or
otherwise gone out of business. Others had unlisted telephone numbers or no telephone at all. New firms had been started as well.

General building contractors accounted for 28 percent of the
businesses identified, although many of these firms were little more
than carpentry contractors working on small remodeling jobs.
Asian-Americans had proportionately highest representation in the
"general building contractor" category, whereas Spanish-American
contractors had the lowest. The strongest black general contracting
firms were found in Atlanta and San Francisco-Oakland. Overall,
the strongest contingent of specialty contractors was found in
Chicago.

Among specialty contractors, patterns show some significant
similarities between cities. Minority contractors are virtually
absent from trades such as elevator and escalator contracting,
highway and street construction, and rare in sheet-metal work,
excavation and grading, glass and glazing, and ironwork (especially
structural ironwork). They are most numerous in painting and
(except among blacks in San Francisco) in carpentry. They are
relatively numerous in plumbing and electrical work.

Beyond these similarities, there are unique local concentra-
tions in selected trades. More than one out of four identified Mexican-American contractors in Houston is a tile contractor. Blacks
in Atlanta are heavily concentrated in masonry, whereas blacks in
Houston are most strongly represented in concrete work. Japanese-
American firms in San Francisco-Oakland are almost exclusively
landscaping contractors.

Of the 1,275 minority construction contractors reportedly
economically active identified in Atlanta, Houston, Chicago, and
San Francisco-Oakland, 315 or 25 percent were interviewed for
this book. Table 2.2 gives a distribution of contractors interviewed
by their construction specialty.

The interview sample provides best coverage among the larger, more established minority contractors. Although Minority-Owned Businesses: 1972 reported fewer than one out of four minority construction firms have paid employees, four out of five contractors interviewed had at least one employee on the payroll. In total, interviews were conducted with 263 contractors with paid employees, or 35 percent of the number of firms with employees found by the census, Minority-Owned Businesses: 1972, in the four metropolitan areas.

CHARACTERISTICS OF CONTRACTORS INTERVIEWED

The most outstanding feature of the population of minority contractors interviewed was their diversity of background, attitudes, capability, and experience. Having interviewed several hundred minority contractors, one would find it difficult to describe a typical minority contractor. Nevertheless, there are some significant patterns that emerge. Some of the patterns vary significantly by minority group, by geographic area, or by type of contractor.

The average current age of the minority contractors interviewed was 45 years (see Table A.1) and they had an average of 10.9 years of experience as contractors. More than seven out of ten had begun their businesses before 1968 when the current efforts to promote "black capitalism" or "minority enterprise" began. Thus, although the data show a strong rate of business formation since 1968, most minority construction enterprises were begun before such efforts were publicly promoted by the Nixon administration.

By and large, the contractors interviewed did not reside in disadvantaged ghetto areas. Outside of San Francisco-Oakland, where the Model Cities area is unusually extensive, only 45 percent of the contractors had either a home or business located within Model Cities boundaries. It would appear from these data that any program aimed exclusively at Model-Cities-area contractors would be doomed to reach few of the existing enterprises (and typically, only the marginal ones).

Many of the general contractors built their businesses by beginning as specialty contractors. Almost without exception, the specialty contractors were craftsmen* before they became contrac-

---

*Where possible, terms without sex connotations have been used throughout this book. However, at editorial suggestion, masculine pronouns were utilized in several places to facilitate continuity in reading. No affront is attended to the two female contractors

TABLE 2.2

Economically Active Contractors Interviewed, by City,
Ethnic/Racial Background, and Specialty

Specialty	Atlanta	Houston			Subtotal, Cities in South	Chicago		
	Black	Black	Spanish-American	Total	South	Black	Spanish-American	Total
General contractors	13	5	8	13	26	4	7	11
Sub or specialty contractors								
Acoustical	—	—	—	—	—	—	—	—
Air conditioning, heating, refrigeration	6	1	6	7	13	3	1	4
Carpentry	5	1	6	7	12	—	4	4
Concrete (including paving)	—	—	1	1	1	1	—	1
Dry wall	2	—	2	2	4	1	—	1
Electrical	4	1	2	3	7	1	3	4
Elevator and escalator	—	—	—	—	—	—	—	—
Excavating and grading	1	—	—	—	1	1	—	1
Floor covering (except wood)	1	—	2	2	3	1	—	1

Floor (wood)	—	—	—	—	—	—	—	—
Glass and glazing	—	—	1	1	1	1	—	1
Hauling (construction materials)	1	1	1	2	2	1	—	—
Insulation	—	—	—	—	—	—	—	1
Ironwork—ornamental, structural, reinforcing, fencing	1	—	1	1	2	3	1	4
Landscaping	—	—	1	1	1	1	—	1
Masonry—brick, block, and stone	7	1	—	1	8	1	—	1
Painting, decorating, paperhanging	3	1	2	3	6	1	—	1
Plastering and lathing	1	—	—	—	1	1	—	1
Plumbing	4	2	5	7	11	3	2	5
Roofing (wood shingle, composition, hand-split shake)	1	—	1	1	2	—	—	—
Sheet metal	—	—	—	—	—	1	—	1
Tile and terrazzo (pre-cast and poured)	2	—	12	12	14	1	—	1
Wrecking and demolition	—	—	—	—	—	1	—	1
Other	—	—	2	2	2	1	—	1
Related trades								
Building maintenance	2	—	—	—	2	—	—	—
TOTAL	53	13	53	66	119	27	18	45

(continued)

(Table 2.2 continued)

	San Francisco-Oakland							Subtotal, Cities in non-South	Total Minorities, All Cities	San Francisco-Oakland Whites
	Black	Spanish-American	Spaniard-American	Chinese-American	Japanese-American	American Indian	Total			
General contractors	27	8	1	10	1	1	48	59	85	11
Sub or specialty contractors										
Acoustical	—	—	—	—	—	—	—	—	—	—
Air conditioning, heating refrigeration	2	2	—	—	—	—	4	8	21	1
Carpentry	1	1	1	—	1	1	5	9	21	—
Concrete (including paving)	5	—	—	—	—	—	5	6	7	—
Dry wall	2	—	—	—	—	—	2	3	7	—
Electrical	9	2	2	4	1	—	18	22	29	2
Elevator and escalator	—	—	—	—	—	—	—	—	—	—
Excavating and grading	4	—	—	—	—	—	4	5	6	—
Floor covering (except wood)	4	—	—	—	—	—	4	5	8	1
Floor (wood)	—	—	—	—	—	—	—	—	—	—
Glass and glazing	1	1	—	—	—	—	2	3	4	1
Hauling (construction materials)	—	—	—	—	—	—	—	—	2	—

Insulation,	—	—	—	—	—	—	—	—	—	—
Ironwork—ornamental, structural, reinforcing, fencing	—	4	1	—	—	—	—	5	9	11	2
Landscaping	—	—	—	—	2	—	—	2	3	4	—
Masonry—brick, block, and stone	1	1	—	—	—	—	—	1	2	10	—
Painting, decorating, paperhanging	14	1	2	3	—	—	—	20	21	27	4
Plastering and lathing	5	1	—	—	—	—	—	6	7	8	—
Plumbing	9	1	1	1	1	—	—	13	18	29	1
Roofing (wood shingle, composition, hand-split shake)	3	1	—	—	—	—	—	4	4	6	1
Sheet metal	—	1	—	—	—	—	—	1	2	2	1
Tile and terrazzo (precast and poured)	2	1	—	—	—	—	—	3	4	18	—
Wrecking and demolition	3	1	—	—	—	—	—	4	5	5	—
Other	—	—	—	—	—	—	—	—	1	3	—
Related trades											
Building maintenance	—	—	—	—	—	—	—	—	—	2	—
TOTAL	92	25	8	18	6	2	—	151	196	315	25

SOURCE: Personal interviews with contractors. Data for Atlanta and Houston were gathered in 1971. Data for Chicago and San Francisco–Oakland were collected during 1973–74.

tors. On the average, these craftsmen-turned-contractors had 21.7 years of experience at their trade.

Training sources for contractors who began as craftsmen are summarized in Table A.6. A majority of those contractors with trades report that they "picked up their trade on the job" without formal training. Formal training sources varied significantly by geographic area. In the non-South cities where union participation was higher, apprenticeship was the most significant formal source of training. In Chicago and San Francisco, 37 percent of the contractors had been trained in apprenticeship. By contrast, in Houston and Atlanta, only 9 percent had served apprenticeships. In the South, the predominant source of formal training was vocational education. Of those interviewed, 38 percent of the southern contractors indicated they had received some training in some form of vocational education; for northern contractors, the comparable figure was only 17 percent. A large portion of the most successful southern black general contractors, as well as those in the plumbing and electrical specialties, learned their skills in black colleges, especially Tuskegee Institute in Alabama. However, only a handful of minority contractors outside the South had learned their trade through a black college.

Patterns of union membership varied significantly by geographic area. (See Table A.12.) The incidence of prior union membership among minority contractors was high in Chicago (69 percent) and San Francisco (76 percent) as opposed to Atlanta (51 percent) and Houston (31 percent). Further, except for participation of Mexican-Americans in Houston pipe-trades unions, membership in the mechanical trades was almost nil in the South. In fact, several southern contractors in the mechanical trades explained that they were initially prompted to go into business for themselves because they could not get into the unions. Somewhat in contrast, in Chicago and San Francisco, slightly more than a third of the contractors with union backgrounds had been members of unions in the mechanical trades.

The fact that minority contractors and subcontractors are—by and large—out of the mainstream of the construction industry is reflected in the record of their membership in trade associations. (See Table A.11.) Overall, 87 of 302 respondents (or 29 percent) stated that they did not belong to any association. An

---

interviewed for this study nor to women who aspire to be contractors. Rather, let these pronouns serve as a nagging reminder that beyond the participation of minorities in the construction industry, full participation by women remains an even more remote dream.

additional 143 contractors (or 47 percent) said that they belonged to minority contractors' associations exclusively. Only 70 contractors (or 23 percent) mentioned holding membership in a nonminority contractors' association.

The few minority contractors belonging to predominantly white associations were usually enthusiastic about the benefits of their membership. Many indicated that these groups were a good way to meet and establish working relationships with white general contractors. Others mentioned the educational benefits of the occasional seminars and lectures sponsored by their organizations. In addition, two minority members of the Associated Building Contractors (ABC) in Houston expressed enthusiasm about labor-training opportunities newly available through their organization. [7]

Generally, the capabilities of the contractors interviewed were limited by their lack of business experience and training, although there were many exceptions and a wide diversity in experience and capabilities among individuals. Overall, only one out of three had business experience and less than a third had business training of any kind before establishing their construction firms. Approximately half of the respondents had neither. (See Table A.4.)

All but a handful of minority contractors interviewed had started their own business (rather than inheriting it), and, as true entrepreneurs, they possess the characteristics attributed to this group by previous studies. Contractors generally founded their businesses at a relatively early age; the average age for founding the firms surveyed was 34.4 years. (See Table A.2.) They are a highly mobile group. Three-quarters of the blacks had moved to their present locations from other places, many from rural areas in the South. An unusually high proportion of the Spanish-American contractors were foreign-born. In general, the contractors tended to be more highly educated than counterparts in the population at large (see Table A.3). The majority of the contractors had a relative in construction (see Table A.9). Although few contractors inherited their business and few had fathers in the same type of business, the majority of the contractors had a father who was self-employed (see Table A.10). [8] These data confirm the hypothesis that a significant role model, who makes the entrepreneurial act credible, is an important variable in stimulating entrepreneurial activity.

There were many common features involved in the initiation of the businesses. There was a high incidence of moonlighting. Of the 315 contractors interviewed, at least 98 had begun their businesses on a part-time basis while they worked at regular jobs. Apparently, moonlighting enables a contractor to gain some experience and test the market before plunging in full-time. Moreover, very few contractors obtained initial capital from outside sources.

Twenty-four (or 10 percent) of the contractors responding had received assistance with initial financing from banks or savings-and-loan institutions. Only 11 of 334 (or 5 percent) of the contractors responding had obtained initial capital from the SBA loan programs. Although other sources—such as customer advances, supplier credit, and loans from family, friends, or previous bosses—were occasionally used, the contractors themselves were by far the primary source of their firms' "start-up" capital. Many of the contractors added that they did not need much capital to get into business, although many suggested that they would have required more if they were to "get into business properly" (that is to be well financed). Finally, the decision to form a business was often influenced by common factors: various positive influences, such as the encouragement and support of a builder or general contractor; or negative influences, such as being denied union membership.

Once established in business, the contractors generally worked only for their own firms. This finding is contrary to conventional wisdom, which contends that minority contractors drift in and out of contracting. It is presumed that they contract when the market is good one day, and go to work as an employee for another contractor the next. The data indicate this assumption to be true only for marginal contractors and moonlighting contractors just starting their businesses. The more established contractors never work for someone else. (See Table A.14.)

CHARACTERISTICS OF THE FIRMS

Type of Work Performed

Overall, almost half of the minority firms were engaged in residential work either exclusively or predominantly, although the pattern varies geographically (see Table A.22). The reliance upon residential construction was slightly heavier in the South than outside it. Fewer black contractors surveyed in Chicago engaged in residential work.

Such heavy reliance on residential construction makes many minority contractors more vulnerable to the frequent downturns in residential construction resulting from changes in the interest rate. Residential construction markets are much more prone to instability than are commercial/industrial markets and this concentration on residential markets makes for greater business risks.

Regarding the government work, 79 percent of the contractors outside the South indicated that they had performed at least one government job by 1973-74. In contrast, only 48 percent of the

southern contractors interviewed in 1971 indicated they had performed any government work. Model Cities and urban-development
projects accounted for a preponderance of the government work performed in all localities. Contracts from state governments were not
mentioned by a single contractor in the South and by only one out of
five contractors outside the South. (The issue of government work
and the minority contractor is treated in greater detail in Chapter
4.)

As illustrated in Table 2.3, most of the contractors in the
cities studied are specialty contractors, and even among those
classified as general contractors, most are remodeling and repair
specialists. Nationally, the Bureau of the Census survey of minority-owned business in 1972 placed 81 percent of the black-owned
construction firms and 83 percent of the classified construction
firms owned by Mexican-Americans in the category of "special
trade contractors."

Income

The bulk of the contractors interviewed were in lower-income
categories (see Table A.1). In terms of annual gross dollar volume
of work performed, 47 percent of the contractors interviewed
grossed $50,000 or less the previous year. (Among the southern
contractors, 60 percent fit into this category.)

The considerable inequality existing among minority firms is
apparent in the data presented in Tables 2.3 and 2.4. Analysis of
the data shows that inequality increased slightly over the period
1969-73. As Table 2.5 reveals, the major factor behind the increasing inequality is the strong (48 percent) increase in income
going to firms in the gross income category of $500,000 or more
in 1969. These data are an indicator of large gains for a few minority firms during the 1969-72 period.

Although there were few exceptions and a wide dispersion in
performance, generally the few minority firms already established
in 1969 (with ten or more employees) had the opportunity to grow
and took advantage of it.

As a final point, the last column in Table 2.4 shows that the
growth in total aggregate income from 1969-72 for all 81 minority
firms responding was 55 percent.[*] The Survey of Minority-Owned

---

[*]The reader should be cautioned that since this is a retro-
spective analysis, it does not take into account firms that went out
of business during the period 1969-72. Considered only are firms

TABLE 2.3

Distribution of Number of Minority Firms among Gross Income
Categories, Chicago and San Francisco-Oakland: 1969 and 1972

Gross Income	1969		1972	
Categories	Total	Percent	Total	Percent
$25,000 or less	23	28.40	17	20.94
25,001-50,000	13	16.05	11	13.58
50,001-75,000	8	9.88	8	9.88
75,001-100,000	12	14.81	8	9.88
100,001-200,000	9	11.11	14	17.28
200,001-500,000	10	12.36	13	16.05
500,001 or more	6	7.41	10	12.36
TOTAL	81	100.00	81	100.00

Note: $X^2=9.56$ at six degrees of freedom significant at 85 percent level.

Source: Personal interviews with minority construction contractors. Data include only firms reporting gross income both in 1969 and in 1972.

TABLE 2.4

Distribution of Gross Income among Gross Income Categories, for
Minority Construction Firms, Chicago and San Francisco-Oakland: 1969 and 1972

Gross Income Categories	1969		1972		Percentage Growth Rate for All Firms, 1969-72
	Income Total (000)	Percent	Income Total (000)	Percent	
$25,000 or less	312	2.1	260	1.0	—
25,001-50,000	517	3.5	411	1.4	—
50,001-75,000	527	3.6	507	1.9	—
75,001-100,000	1,045	7.0	730	2.7	—
100,001-200,000	1,459	9.8	2,110	7.8	—
200,001-500,000	3,509	23.6	4,539	16.8	—
500,001 or more	7,500	50.4	18,500	68.4	—
TOTAL	14,869	100.0	27,057	100.0	55

Source: Personal interviews with minority contractors during 1973-74. Data include only firms reporting gross income both in 1969 and in 1972.

TABLE 2.5

Distribution of Average Income among Gross Income Categories for
Minority Construction Firms, Chicago and San Francisco-Oakland: 1969 and 1972

Gross Income Categories	1969	1972	Percentage Change, 1969-72
$25,000 or less	14	15	7.1
25,001-50,000	40	37	(-7.5)
50,001-75,000	66	63	(-4.6)
75,001-100,000	87	91	4.9
100,001-200,000	162	151	(-6.8)
200,001-500,000	351	349	(- .6)
500,000 or more	1,250	1,850	48.0

Source: Personal interviews with minority contractors during 1973-74. Data include only firms reporting gross income both in 1969 and 1972.

24

<u>Business Enterprises</u> found that average receipts per firm rose from 1969-72 by 42 percent for black-owned firms, 32 percent for firms owned by Mexican-Americans, and 37 percent for minority firms as a whole. [9] For the sake of comparison, it is instructive to note that the rate of growth in reported total domestic contracts of firms named on the <u>Engineering News-Record</u> "Top 400 Listing" rose only 32 percent from 1969-72. Further, among the top ten firms, the growth rate was 26 percent. [10]

Employment

Considerable inequality existed in the distribution of number of employees on the payroll among minority firms interviewed. In fact, 20 percent of the black and Spanish-American firms accounted for more than 70 percent of the total employment among firms interviewed. Among other Asian-American and American Indian firms, the inequality was not as predominant; 20 percent of the firms accounted for just over 50 percent of total employment.

Among 293 minority firms responding in the four Standard Metropolitan Statistical Areas (SMSAs), there were 43 (or 15 percent) with no employees at all. An additional 116 firms (or 40 percent) had only one to three employees. At the other end of the scale, 62 firms (or 21 percent) had ten or more employees. Only four firms (or 1 percent) had 50 or more employees (see Table A. 27).

According to aggregate census data, minority firms in the four SMSAs employed only a small fraction of the construction labor force in those labor markets. As illustrated in Table 2. 6, employment by minority firms at best accounted for only 3 percent of the total employment in contract construction.

However, aggregate census data are deceptive and may understate the employment-generating potential of minority contractors in particular trades and particular local labor markets. Our information revealed important differences by trade and place. For example, although the overall percentage of construction workers employed in minority shops in the San Francisco-Oakland SMSA amounted to only 2.1 percent in 1972, the total peak employment of minority electrical contractors in the Oakland area during

---

in business both in 1969 and 1972. However, since there is no evidence to indicate that larger firms went out of business at greater rates than smaller firms (rather the opposite), the conclusion drawn from limited analysis should not be overturned.

TABLE 2.6

Employment in Minority Firms as
a Percentage of Total Employment In
Contract Construction by SMSA: 1969 and 1972

SMSA and Year	Total Employment in Contract Construction	Total Number Employed by Minority Firms	Employment in Minority Firms as a Percent of Total Employment in Contract Construction
Atlanta			
1969	35,700	487	1.4
1972	39,800	1018	2.6
Chicago			
1969	127,800	510	0.4
1972	119,200	1006	2.6
Houston			
1969	66,800	989	1.5
1972	67,700	2036	3.0
San Francisco- Oakland			
1969	62,700	846	1.4
1972	59,200	1232	2.1

Source: Data on total employment in contract construction was taken from Bureau of Labor Statistics, Employment and Earnings: States and Areas 1939-72, Bulletin 1370-10 (Washington, D. C.: Government Printing Office, 1974). Data on 1969 employment in minority firms came from U.S. Bureau of the Census, Minority-Owned Businesses: 1969, Report MB-1 (Washington, D. C.: Government Printing Office, 1971), table 6. Data on 1972 employment in minority firms was calculated from U.S. Bureau of the Census, 1972 Survey of Minority-Owned Business Enterprises, 4 vols. (Washington, D.C.: Government Printing Office, 1974), table 3.

the period approximately 1969-74 amounted to 108 workers—equivalent to 10.8 percent of the reported total membership of 1,000 in Oakland International Brotherhood of Electrical Workers (IBEW) Local 595 in 1971-72.[11] In contrast, the nine reportedly active minority plumbing contractors in Atlanta in 1971 employed an estimated peak of 19 workers, a figure equal to 1.9 percent of the total membership of 1,000 in the Atlanta Plumbers and Steamfitters Local 72.[12] Furthermore, all but one of these contractors were 55 years of age or older—an unlikely group of candidates for upgrading.

It is clear, then, that the potential for upgrading minority firms in construction and for utilizing them to help integrate building-trades unions varies by place, trade, and time.

Racial Composition of Employment

According to responses by minority contractors, 1,343 out of 2,234.5, or 60 percent of the total number of employees currently on the payroll, were minority, The tendency for minority contractors to hire minority employees varied somewhat by racial/ ethnic background. It was highest among Asian-Americans (71 percent), then blacks (62 percent), and lowest among Spanish-Americans (53 percent).

Although, on average, all the above figures were considerably above the minority work-force percentages for the white contractors in San Francisco interviewed (30 percent), affirmative-action officers interviewed pointed out several examples of individual Anglo-owned firms that employed larger percentages of minority workers than did competing minority firms.[13]

One of the striking impressions made by interviews and initial casual examination of the data was that the larger the minority firm, the larger was its proportion of nonminority workers. It may be reasoned that as a minority contractor grows and expands his work force, he tends to rely on sources of labor outside the minority community, such as union hiring halls. To check this observation more carefully, the rank correlation of size of firm to proportion of minorities in the work force was computed, with the following results:

Racial/Ethnic Group	R^{2*}
Other nonwhites (Asian-American, American Indians)	-.17
Blacks	-.33
Spanish-Americans	-.49

*The values are significant at the 99 percent level for blacks and Spanish-Americans. For other nonwhites, the value is significant at the 60 percent level.

Thus, a strong but not complete negative correlation holds between firm size of minority firms and the proportion of minority workers. It is strongest among Spanish-American firms, then blacks, and finally Asian-American firms.

Regional Differences

Significant differences exist between patterns in southern cities and in Chicago and San Francisco.

Perhaps most strikingly, more than nine out of ten minority firms in the South were nonunion, whereas three out of four firms outside the South were unionized (see Table A.17). Minority contractors in heavily unionized environments operated union shops themselves. There were only two exceptions to this non-South pattern—Spanish-American contractors in Chicago, who, as a group, were very disadvantaged, and Chinese-American contractors in San Francisco, who worked in historically nonunion China-town.

Interestingly, when asked about unions, a few of the southern contractors expressed desire to become unionized but felt it was currently impossible. One interviewee—a Mexican-American plumbing contractor—had worked under a union contract but dropped it after a couple of years when he could not find sufficient contracts to support the union wages he was paying. Another contractor responded to the question. "Do you operate a union shop?" with the remark, "I wish I were into that gravy! But I couldn't find enough good jobs to support it."

A second major difference was that while not a single joint venture between a black and white firm was found in the South, such an experience was relatively common among minority contractors in the non-South (16 percent had joint-ventured with a white firm; see Table A.39).

Third, southern minority contractors were more likely to work exclusively or primarily in residential construction markets than their northern counterparts (see Table A.22) and less likely to participate in government work (see Table A.23).

Fourth, contractors in Houston and Atlanta were more concentrated in lower income and employment categories than contractors in Chicago and San Francisco. For example, 41 percent of the contractors in the South grossed $25,000 or less, whereas only 25 percent of the contractors outside the South were in this category. And 59 percent of southern contractors had three or fewer employees, whereas among their counterpart respondents, 51 percent had three or fewer employees.

Fifth, greater proportions of contractors in the South tended to operate informally. For example, 19 percent of minority contractors in the South reported that they relied predominantly on verbal contracts. (See Table A.19.) Among black and Spanish-heritage contractors outside the South, the comparable figure was only 9 percent (Asian-American contractors—perhaps for cultural reasons—tended to follow the pattern found among the southern contractors). Another indicator of the informality among southern firms was the incidence of those who did not carry liability or workers' compensation insurance. Whereas 34 of 104 respondents (or 33 percent) in the southern cities reported not carrying any insurance at all, only 10 of 181 respondents in the non-South reported having no insurance (see Table A.20). Of the southern contractors interviewed, approximately 10 percent operated without business license or registration of any kind. This in effect made their business illegal and put them in an unfavorable position in setting their prices. Southern contractors were also more likely to operate out of their homes (see Table A.18), and operate without benefit of corporate status (see Table A.16), and were more likely to rely on informal sources for jobs and labor (see Tables A.35 and A.36).

Finally, southern contractors were much more likely than their counterparts in Chicago and San Francisco to rely on themselves for financing rather than applying to a financial institution (see Table A.29) and much less likely to have applied for bonding (Table A.33).

PROBLEMS OF SPANISH-AMERICAN AND ASIAN-AMERICAN CONTRACTORS

Spanish-American contractors were generally at greater disadvantage than blacks. They typically had smaller businesses, were less well informed about government programs such as the SBA assistance efforts, had less prior training or business experience, operated their businesses more informally, and were less likely to have formal training programs for their employees. The contrasts were especially marked in Chicago and Houston.

The problems of the Spanish-American are further complicated because many Spanish-Americans who have succeeded no longer identify with their minority group. Two of the most prosperous of the Mexican-American contractors in Houston revealed this attitude:

> They [the Mexican American Contractors Association (MACA)] have the wrong approach. Even using the name "Mexican-American" is self-defeating. We

are of Mexican extraction and that is as far as it goes.
They don't seem to realize they are American before
anything else.

I don't believe in the MACA approach. That is
segregating yourself. It is just like the Mexican-
American Chamber of Commerce. Why not join the
regular chamber of commerce?

Some less prosperous contractors also expressed the same
viewpoint. As one Mexican-American in Houston stated: "They
[MACA] never help me. I don't think they can help me. I am an
American and I can get work if I need it. . . . I may have to go a
little lower on price, but I can get it."

Among Asian-American contractors in San Francisco, Japanese contractors interviewed were more established than Chinese
contractors in terms of gross income, size of largest contract performed, number of employees, degree of unionization, and other
indicators. Many Chinese contractors did not speak English and consequently were confined to working with Chinese customers. Several
others operate nonunion shops (Chinese contractors are the least
unionized of any minority in the San Francisco area). To avoid union
organization pressures, they operate exclusively in Chinatown. Many
Chinese contractors were reluctant to undertake government jobs,
for fear of encountering union pressures.* They reasoned that if
they became unionized and paid union wage rates, they would become
noncompetitive in Chinatown where their "bread-and-butter" jobs
were located. One of the chief aims of ASIAN, Inc., an economic
development corporation that assists Asian-American businessmen
in the Bay area, was to encourage and assist the more qualified contractors to risk performing jobs outside of Chinatown, thus over-
coming the barriers that a limited minority market presents to
growth.[14]

SUMMARY AND CONCLUSIONS

From the present survey and previous studies and surveys
made by the NAACP, Shapiro, and the U.S. Bureau of the Census,[15]
the following conclusions about minority contractors may be drawn:

Although it is now known that there are more minority firms
in construction than was estimated in 1969, minority contractors
are relatively few in number and are typically small enterprises.
In fact, the large, successful minority contractor is such a rarity
that he is a news item.[16]

---

*The sole exception to this statement appears to be work on
military bases, where unions are forbidden to picket.

The drive to promote minority capitalism in the late 1960s and early 1970s shows mixed results in construction. Data collected in Chicago and San Francisco indicate that many larger firms —those with ten or more employees—have benefited from the opportunities made available during this period.[*] Unfortunately, however, these firms constitute only a tiny portion of minority enterprise in construction. Medium-sized firms—those with three to nine employees—show smaller gains, but their work volumes nevertheless grew almost twice as fast over the period 1969-72 as the volumes of the top 400 firms in construction (cited in Engineering News-Record). The smallest firms (zero to two employees)—the most numerous classification—reported the smallest gains. In summary, it appears that the promotion of minority capitalism has benefited a few of the larger contractors but has left the bulk of firms in relatively the same position they occupied before it all began.

Most minority firms operate outside of the mainstream of the construction industry and do not have high visibility. The majority interviewed did not advertise and were not listed in the yellow pages of the telephone book. Only 23 percent of the contractors held memberships in nonminority trade associations. Sixty-one percent of the contractors worked out of their homes rather than an office.

Significant contrasts between minority contractors in the South and non-South exist. Southern minority contractors were almost totally nonunion, whereas three out of four non-South contractors interviewed were unionized. Joint ventures between minority and nonminority firms were totally absent in the South, whereas 16 percent of minority contractors outside the South had participated in at least one such venture. Southern contractors also tended to do more residential work and were less likely to have performed any government jobs. Greater proportions of contractors in Houston and Atlanta operated their firms on an informal basis and had not applied for bonding or bank loans.

Almost without exception, minority specialty contractors came to contracting through a trade. However, there appear to be other routes to general contracting, such as engineering, architecture, and real estate. Although the contractors tended to be more highly educated than their counterparts in the city population, their capabilities as contractors were often limited owing to their lack of business experience and training.

---

[*]Not all the larger contractors have gained, of course. There have been some dramatic casualties owing to overextension along the way, such as the Winston Burnett Corporation of New York City and Jackie Robinson's Corporation in Boston.

Although these generalizations are by and large true, minority construction contractors as individuals fit no stereotypes. They range in talent from the illiterate linoleum layer with no formal schooling who subcontracts his own labor and determines how much he has laid each day by counting the number of boxes of tiles he has emptied to the electrical contractor with a graduate degree in electrical engineering who designs and installs complex electrical systems for commercial buildings. Nor are all minority contractors hard-working honest men who would do much better if only they could become unshackled from the chains of discrimination. Many have the ability and desire to be doing much better than they currently are. But some with lesser talents would not be able to utilize opportunities if they had them, and some would only dig themselves into deeper trouble if they tried to take on such opportunities. Nevertheless, some have the potential to take on more work, larger work, or better work; but they confront certain obstacles to these goals.

NOTES

1.   G. Douglas Pugh, "Bonding Minority Contractors," in Black Economic Development, ed. William F. Haddad and G. Douglas Pugh (Englewood Cliffs, N. J.: Prentice-Hall, 1969) p. 139.

2.   Joseph Debro, "The Minority Builder," Labor Law Journal 21 (May 1970): 298.

3.   U.S. Department of Housing and Urban Development, Office of the Assistant Secretary for Equal Opportunity, Registry of Minority Construction Contractors (Washington, D.C.: Government Printing Office, 1970). The Registry contains names, addresses, and other information on the 2,051 contractors interviewed.

4.   Small Business Administration, as cited in Ronald W. Bailey, "Introduction/Black Enterprise: Reflections on Its History and Future Development," in Black Business Enterprise: Historical and Contemporary Perspectives, ed. Ronald W. Bailey (New York: Basic Books, 1971) p. 8.

5.   The 870,000 figure is taken from the Bureau of the Census. The SBA working estimate of 8,000 is cited in U.S. Department of Housing and Urban Development, Office of the Assistant Secretary for Equal Opportunity, A Survey of Minority Construction Contractors (Washington, D.C.: Government Printing Office, 1971), p. 1.

6.   See, for example, Department of Housing and Urban Development, Registry of Minority Construction Contractors, p. 5.

7.   See "Open Shop Apprenticeship Programs Approved," Engineering News-Record, June 10, 1971, p. 68.

8.   This finding concurs with other studies on the subject. Lewis D. Davids, Characteristics of Small Business Founders in Texas and Georgia (Washington, D.C.: University of Georgia for the Small Business Administration, 1963), found more than 50 percent of parents self-employed in both states. Orvis F. Collins, David G. Moore, and Darob B. Unwalla, Enterprising Man (East Lansing: Bureau of Business and Economic Research, Graduate School of Business Administration, Michigan State University, 1964), found 25 percent of fathers self-employed and an additional 19 percent of them farmers. Edward B. Roberts and Herbert A. Wainer, "Technological Transfer and Entrepreneurial Success," paper presented at the 20th National Conference on the Administration of Research, October 27, 1966, Miami Beach, Florida, found 50 percent of fathers self-employed. Kirk Draheim, Richard P. Howell, and Albert Shapero, The Development of a Potential Defense R&D Complex: A Study of Minneapolis-St. Paul, R&D Studies Series (Menlo Park, Calif.: Stanford Research Institute, 1966), concluded that the father "in many instances" was himself an entrepreneur or executive.

9.   Calculated from U.S. Bureau of the Census, 1972 Survey of Minority-Owned Business Enterprises, Special Report MB-72 (Washington, D.C.: Government Printing Office, 1975), table 1. The term "minority" included black, Spanish origin, Asian-American, American Indian, and other nonwhites.

10.   Data calculated from Engineering News-Record, April 9, 1970 and April 12, 1973.

11.   Total union membership figures are cited in Ray Marshall, William S. Franklin, and Robert W. Glover, Training and Entry into Union Construction (Washington, D.C.: Government Printing Office, 1975), table 14. It must be cautioned however, that not all employees of these minority electrical firms were journeymen electricians. Some were clerical workers, laborers, or electricians' helpers.

12.   Ibid., table 22.

13.   Personal interviews with Chet V. Brookins, labor relations and EEO officer, Henry C. Beck Company, San Francisco, January 28, 1974, and with Stanley Lim, employment representative, Human Rights Commission of San Francisco, May 16, 1972.

14.   Personal interview with John Schulman, business consultant, ASIAN, Inc., San Francisco, December 20, 1973.

15.   Department of Housing and Urban Development, A Survey of Minority Construction Contractors; Theresa R. Shapiro, "Black Builders in Greater New Orleans," Louisiana Business Review 2 (July 1971): 10-12; U.S. Bureau of the Census, Minority-Owned Business: 1969, Report MB-1 (Washington, D.C.: Government Printing Office, 1971).

16.   See, for example, the cover story on New York City's F. W. Eversley, "Fred W. Eversley Aims for the Top," Engineering News-Record, July 31, 1969, pp. 47-48; or more recently, the cover story, "A Successful Black Contractor's Advice on How to Succeed: Get Big," Engineering News-Record, September 9, 1971, pp. 18-19. Or see the front-page article on Winston A. Burnett by David DuPues, "Harlem-Based Concern Dents a White Preserve, the Construction Field," Wall Street Journal, November 3, 1969. Similarly, see "John W. Winters: Home-Building Contractor," in John Seder and Berkeley G. Burrell, Getting it Together (New York: Harcourt Brace Jovanovich, 1971), pp. 84-104.

3

**OBSTACLES TO
UPGRADING THE
MINORITY CONTRACTOR**

Minority contractors face a multitude of problems in expanding their businesses. Interviews with the contractors were designed to try to identify the contractors' problems and to elicit information about them. Contractors were requested to specify the problems they face in attempting to expand their businesses, and, if possible, to rank the principal three in order of importance. A summary of the responses is shown in Table 3.1. The answers were unprompted, and the tables show a classification of open-ended responses.

The results in the cities studied show similar patterns, especially for those problems most often mentioned. In all cities, financing—especially interim financing—was by far the chief concern of most contractors. The second most prevalent concern was labor, especially finding and keeping qualified workers. Lack of management skills followed as the third most important concern. A few contractors in each of the cities were concerned with bonding.

For some of the less often mentioned problems, patterns varied considerably by city. For example, although marketing (finding jobs) was identified as a severe problem by twenty-nine contractors in San Francisco-Oakland and six in Houston, none of Atlanta's black contractors and only one minority contractor in Chicago mentioned it. Likewise, cheap competition was noted to be a problem in San Francisco-Oakland by sixteen contractors and six in Houston, two in Atlanta, and one in Chicago.

Each problem area was probed in depth with the use of supplementary questions. Experience of the contractors was solicited. If they were successful in dealing with the problem, they were asked how they did it. If they encountered severe difficulties, they were asked to elaborate on their experiences.

TABLE 3.1

Chief Problems of Construction Contractors, as Reported by Contractors
by City and Ethnic/Racial Background

	Atlanta	Houston			Subtotal, Cities in South	Chicago		
	Black	Black	Spanish-American	Total		Black	Spanish-American	Total
Finances								
Finances in general	16	6	10	16	32	1	4	5
Obtaining interim financing	10	3	10	13	23	18	9	27
Meeting capital requirements	3	1	2	3	6	—	1	1
Obtaining credit from suppliers	—	—	2	2	2	1	1	2
Customers have difficulty obtaining financing	1	—	1	1	2	1	—	1
Labor								
Labor in general	8	—	6	6	14	—	—	—
Recruitment	12	6	1	7	19	—	—	—
Recruitment—supervisory personnel	—	—	—	—	—	1	1	2
Turnover	—	—	1	1	1	1	—	1
Difficulties with union	1	—	—	—	1	—	—	—
Training	1	—	—	—	1	—	—	—
Aged work force	1	—	—	—	1	—	—	—

Lack of management skills								
Lack of management skills in general	5	3	—	3	8	4	2	6
Lack of knowledge of financing	1	—	—	—	1	—	—	—
Supervision of personnel	1	—	1	1	2	3	—	3
Estimating and bidding	—	—	5	5	5	—	3	3
Bookkeeping	—	—	1	1	1	1	—	1
Marketing	—	2	7	9	9	—	3	3
Debt Collection	4	1	7	8	12	3	—	3
Cheap Competition	2	—	6	6	8	—	1	1
Bonding	6	3	3	6	12	3	2	5
Discrimination	2	—	—	—	2	—	—	—
Licensing	—	—	—	—	—	—	1	1
Inflation of supply prices	—	—	—	—	—	—	—	—
Other problems	2	—	4	4	6	3	2	6
No problems	2	—	2	2	4	1	2	3
Total respondents	49	12	34	46	95	30	15	45

(continued)

(Table 3.1 continued)

| | San Francisco-Oakland | | | | | | Sub To- tal, Cities in non- South | Total Mi- norities, All Cities | San Francisco- Oakland Whites |
	Black and Indian*	Spanish- American	Spaniard American	Chinese- American	Japanese- American	Total			
Finances									
Finances in general	38	5	3	3	—	49	54	86	7
Obtaining interim financing	49	7	4	1	—	61	88	111	4
Meeting capital requirements	6	2	—	1	—	9	10	16	2
Obtaining credit from suppliers	—	1	—	—	—	1	3	5	1
Customers have diffi- culty obtaining fi- nancing	—	—	—	—	—	—	1	3	—
Labor									
Labor in general	5	—	3	5	—	13	13	27	4
Recruitment	19	2	2	3	—	26	26	45	2
Recruitment—super- visory personnel	4	—	1	3	3	11	13	13	1
Turnover	3	1	—	—	—	4	5	6	2
Difficulties with union	8	—	2	1	1	11	11	12	1
Training	7	—	1	1	—	10	10	11	1
Aged work force	—	—	—	—	—	—	—	1	—

Lack of management skills									
Lack of management skills in general	12	5	—	2	1	20	26	34	—
Lack of knowledge of financing	—	—	—	—	—	—	—	1	—
Supervision of personnel	2	—	—	—	—	2	5	7	1
Estimating and bidding	1	—	—	1	—	2	5	10	1
Bookkeeping	3	1	—	—	—	4	5	6	—
Marketing	19	5	2	2	1	29	32	41	2
Debt Collection	4	2	2	—	—	8	11	23	1
Cheap Competition	8	3	4	1	—	16	17	25	2
Bonding	15	—	—	3	—	18	23	35	—
Discrimination	8	—	—	—	—	8	8	10	1
Licensing	—	—	—	—	—	—	1	1	—
Inflation of supply prices	6	1	1	1	—	9	12	11	6
Other problems	12	15	—	15	1	43	49	53	11
No problems	18	6	2	—	2	28	31	35	5
Total respondents	88	23	7	17	7	142	182	282	25

*This column includes the responses from one American Indian contractor.

Source: Personal interviews with contractors. Data for Atlanta and Houston were gathered in 1971. Data for Chicago and San Francisco—Oakland were collected during 1973–74.

FINANCING

Obtaining finances was identified most frequently by contractors in both cities as their primary business problem. Cited most often was the matter of obtaining interim financing to cover costs of materials and payrolls until the first payment (or "draw") for the job is made. One black general contractor in Atlanta claimed that most of his minority subcontractors could not last more than a week without a draw.

Inability to obtain interim financing limits the operations of minority contractors in several respects. It often prevents a minority contractor from obtaining a job or from undertaking it once the contract is in hand. An undercapitalized air-conditioning contractor in Atlanta lamented, "I have to turn down jobs, such as one this morning, because I have bought all the equipment supplies I can this week." Forty-two contractors in Chicago and the San Francisco area stated that they had turned down large jobs because they could not finance them. Unavailability of financing certainly restricts the type of work a minority contractor is able to perform. Without adequate financing, a contractor must avoid jobs that pay off slowly or contracts on which there is provision for a retainage (usually 10 percent). Most commercial and government construction falls into such categories. As one contractor said, "I can't do government work because I cannot wait long for payment. Even FHA [Federal Housing Authority] repossession work is slow-paying." Pressed for funds, some minority contractors are forced to rely on customer advance or supplier credit, which further limits their effective market. Many underfinanced contractors cannot work at capacity. One Houston contractor, who related that he could not obtain a bank loan although he had excellent personal credit, observed, "I spend more time begging people for money than I do working. We operate on a shoestring." Unavailability of financing can prevent a subcontractor from supplying his own materials, thus reducing the profitability of his jobs. Inability to obtain interim financing is also often related to other problems, such as the inability to secure bonding or the inability to obtain a good work force.

Lack of financing for equipment was also a primary problem. Most minority contractors are undercapitalized—even for small residential construction. For commercial construction, financial needs are even greater—more and different (and usually more expensive) equipment is required. For example, in masonry, lifts and scaffolding are vital in working on multistory buildings. If a minority firm cannot find the money to buy or lease such equipment, it is effectively excluded from the market.

Obtaining financing for equipment, of course, is much more of a problem in the trades for which much equipment is required. Sheet-metal work or poured terrazzo flooring are prime examples. In trades that require little equipment, such as tile and precast terrazzo, the problem of capital financing was rarely mentioned.

Besides interim financing and financing for equipment, other financial problems were mentioned by individual contractors. Sometimes the inability of the contractor's customer to obtain financing becomes a problem for the contractor, especially for those contractors who work in the minority market. One contractor in Atlanta, for example, alleged that it is almost impossible to obtain a FHA guarantee for a loan over $25,000 in a black neighborhood; this, he contends, limits the work he can do. Similarly, a Mexican-American air-conditioning contractor in Houston stated that he would be busy all the time if his customers had access to financing for the installation of air conditioning.

Another problem mentioned by a few contractors is obtaining supplier credit. This issue is most important when a business is first becoming established. Some contractors have arranged a cosignature agreement, in which the customer makes all checks in the name of both the supplier and the contractor, to obtain supplier credit. However, this practice is discouraged by many suppliers and thus is infrequently used.

Few contractors begin their business with assistance from financial institutions. Out of 234 contractors in all cities, only 24 (or 10 percent) identified banks or savings-and-loan associations as sources of their start-up capital. Most contractors provided the initial start-up capital themselves

In most minority firms, the contractors themselves remain the primary source of business funding even after their businesses become established. As one Houston contractor put it, "My largest source of funding is my back pocket." Overall, 147 of 259 respondents (or 57 percent) reported their main source of financing as themselves. Eighty-six (or 33 percent) identified financial institutions as their primary source. Ten (or 4 percent) cited the SBA as the chief source of financing. A few existed on customer advances or financing from white partners. One contractor explained that he managed to exist between draws on larger jobs by doing smaller jobs for which he was paid immediately.

Some significant differences between respondents from the South and non-South existed on this question. Among blacks in Chicago and all minorities in San Francisco-Oakland, almost twice the proportion of respondents relied on financial institutions for operating funds. And all of the contractors who cited the SBA as their chief source of financing were outside the South, but this is probably because the SBA's "revokable, revolving line of credit program" was not in effect at the time of the interviews in the South.

Also attesting to the larger role financial institutions played in supporting contractors in the non-South is the fact that larger percentages of nonsouthern respondents had tried to obtain a bank loan. Whereas 63 percent of the contractors interviewed in Houston or Atlanta had sought a bank loan at one time or another, the comparable figure for non-South respondents was 74 percent.

In all cities, blacks applied for bank business loans more than other minorities. Of the black respondents, 80 percent had applied for bank loans, whereas only 56 percent of the nonblack minorities had done so. The most aggressive contractors in seeking bank loans were blacks in Chicago. Twenty-four out of 26 contractors (or 92 percent) had applied for bank loans—with an 85 percent success rate.

However, even for this group, the future looked bleak. In final interviews conducted in April 1974 during the credit crunch, much concern was expressed by Chicago contractors about the future availability and price of credit. As small contractors, they were increasingly finding themselves at the end of the line in obtaining credit. The future outlook posed a dilemma. If they could not get credit, they could not bid for jobs and work; and if they could get credit, it was at a high price that cut deeply into profits. One contractor summed up the problem: "How can I make profits paying 14 to 18 percent interest rates?"

Overall, 81 percent or about four out of five contractors who have applied for a bank loan had been successful at least once. Lower rates of success were found among blacks in Atlanta and San Francisco-Oakland and among Spanish-Americans in Chicago.

Several contractors who had been refused in initial applications were eventually successful in obtaining a loan. Such experience testifies to the value of persistence in dealing with lending institutions.

Surprisingly, minority contractors make relatively little use of minority banks, and the presence of such minority-owned institutions does not appear to ease contractors' financial problems much. Few minority contractors reported carrying accounts with minority banks, and less than a handful considered a minority-owned financial institution to be their chief source of financing. When asked why, one Mexican-American contractor in Houston responded, "[A Mexican-American bank] just recently opened, and since they want to stay in business, I heard that they are—understandably—more

conservative about their loan policies than some white banks are. "
The contractor was hopeful for a more open policy when the bank
becomes more firmly established.

Even in Chicago, where some of the largest black financial
institutions are located, contractors made little use of such estab-
lishments. A black contractor in Chicago simply stated: "Minority
banks don't have the money. " A fellow contractor added: "They
don't have the expertise to get involved in high risk, short-term
construction loans. They have their money tied up in long-term
mortgages and such. "

Interestingly, of the contractors who had established good
financial credit with banks, several had personal contacts or
friends at the bank or developed such relationships over time. In
Houston, many of the inmigrant contractors still used their rural
hometown banks where they "know the vice-president" or where
they "are well known" rather than dealing with the major Houston
banks. One Atlanta black carpentry contractor stated that he had
been offered a loan only once—when he was doing some carpentry
work on the offering bank's office. The majority of contractors
lack such business contacts with bankers, however.

At least some of the lack of contact between minority contractors and financial institutions can be attributed to the paucity of
minority bank-loan officers. For example, a survey made in 1969
preliminary to the charter application for the Pan American National
Bank found a total of only three Mexican-American loan officers
working in Houston banks. [1]

Where minority loan officers were to be found in Houston and
other cities, the minority contractors seemed to gravitate to them;
it was not unusual for the same minority loan officer in a white-
owned bank to handle accounts with several minority contractors.
Minority contractor associations often gained entry to financing for
their membership through minority loan officers because "they
could speak the language" or because "they had rapport. " Thus, an
effective affirmative-action program on the part of white banks to
hire more minority loan officers would be of considerable assistance
in reducing problems of financing for minority contractors.

Established credit is a requirement for any substantial construction enterprise; and it must often be available on very short
notice to meet a bid deadline or to keep a firm afloat during unex-
pected delays or unforeseen reverses. A black contractor in Chicago
lamented:

The trouble is that whites have an advantage in that
they can pick up the phone and operate by word of
mouth—even get same-day service. Blacks haven't

established themselves with banks to be able to
do this yet and although this may happen tomorrow sometime, we don't have till tomorrow to
do it.

LABOR

As noted in Table 3.1, labor was the second most prevalent
problem area cited by the contractors, although it received only
about half as much attention as financing. Four main issues were
cited: recruitment; retention; training; and relationships with
unions.

Recruitment

Finding labor was mentioned as a major problem 58 times by
the 282 contractors. In order to obtain a fuller picture of this problem, each contractor was asked directly and specifically, "Do you
have any trouble finding and keeping reliable and capable workers?"
Overall, 134 of 272 contractors (or 49 percent) responded affirmatively. Many added that inferior or unskilled workers were available,
but skilled craftsworkers were difficult to find.

The nature of the contractors' labor problems seems to change
as the firm grows and develops. Three out of four minority firms
in construction nationally do not have even one person on the payroll
and therefore have no recruitment worries. When the firm grows
and a work force is hired, a contractor becomes concerned with
keeping his better craftsworkers—which usually means he has to
keep them busy. As he grows larger, his need for skilled craftsworkers increases, as does his concern for recruiting and training
them. If the contractor achieves a more stable level of work and
becomes unionized, his labor recruitment and training problems
diminish because he can rely on union referral. The critical need
then becomes attracting competent supervisory personnel.

Finding such personnel is a particularly sticky problem for
some of the larger contractors. Most of the black contractors have
difficulty attracting white supervisors, and blacks with supervisory
skills are in short supply because few have been trained. Furthermore, many of those who have suitable experience prefer to work
for white firms at higher salaries or to go into business for themselves. As one black contractor in Chicago described his problem:
"I would like to find a minority guy with an engineering background
who has a practical understanding of the trades as well as an ability
to deal with people. I guess I just asked for Jesus Christ—and I
despair of a second coming."

The contractors were also asked how they found workers (see Table A.31). Sources were numerous and diverse. In the South, contractors use informal sources almost exclusively whereas contractors outside the South rely heavily on union referral.

Various forms of informal sources were used by the contractors, especially calling acceptable former employees. Some contractors keep a list of such employees. Many attempt to hire only employees of whose competence they know personally. Most contractors also prefer to hire only experienced workers instead of hiring the unskilled and enduring the difficulties of training them; but as "greenhorns" are often the only labor available, they have no choice but to employ and train them. Other informal channels include recommendations of friends or relatives, referrals from fellow contractors or from employees, hiring "walk-ins," picking up people at street corner "shape-ups" (especially in Atlanta), hiring neighborhood youngsters, or employing former workers who call when they are out of work. In painting and tile contracting, wholesale suppliers sometimes act as referral sources for labor. Informal networks provide advantages to contractors who have long been well established in the area either as workers or employers. Such contractors simply know more people. Nonunion contractors new to the business often encounter severe problems finding capable and reliable labor.

Eleven contractors in the South and 103 contractors in the non-South mention that they use union halls or union referral systems to obtain workers. Generally, in the non-South, only union shops use union referral. However, in the South, four of the eleven contractors are nonunion and use the union referral without a contract, although they said that they are obligated to pay the union scale. Moreover, not all of the unionized contractors in the South used union referral. Atlanta's largest black union contractor claimed he had not used union referral in seven years. "Workers come to me," he said, "because they know I have work all year round, which means a steady job and more security for them." Further, if a nonunion contractor in the South has a large work force and pays a wage near union rates, union workers will call on him looking for work, especially during strikes.

Several contractors criticized the quality of workers the union had referred them. Some contractors contended that workers who "hang around" the union hall relying on the referral system for jobs are older or less productive or otherwise inferior workers. A few contractors charged that they had been discriminated against in union referrals. Other contractors explained simply that the largest employers carried the most weight with the unions and thus got the best referrals; and minority contractors are generally not among these largest firms. Another contractor also noted that inferior workers are often dispatched to out-of-town contractors who are in the local labor market only temporarily.

A few contractors mentioned use of the public employment service to find employees. However, most see it as a source for laborers but never for skilled workers. Generally, minority contractors do not give the employment service high ratings: for every contractor who spoke favorably of the service, two made negative comments.

Besides union referral and the employment service, other formal sources were rarely used. Few contractors had established connections with trade schools for obtaining workers. Half of those who did were contractors in Atlanta who hired graduates from the Atlanta Area Technical School. In other cities, there was little or no relationship with any vocational-education facilities for obtaining workers. Newspaper or radio/TV advertisements were used by only a handful of firms, largely Spanish-speaking contractors utilizing Spanish-speaking media.

Finding and keeping workers is enough of a problem to keep some contractors—especially nonunion contractors—out of the line of work they want to do, as illustrated by the following sample quotations:

> Yes, I have had offers to do nonresidential work, but I don't have the work force.
> (Black general remodeling contractor, Atlanta)

> My work has been 90 percent remodeling lately because I can't find enough men to do new work.
> (Black general contractor, Atlanta)

> I used to do commercial work—but I couldn't find enough good men. . . . I went broke.
> (Black general contractor, Houston)

> We have had to turn down jobs because we have had no workers.
> (Black electrical contractor, Atlanta)

> I used to do a lot of new installation work but I had to go to service and other less quality work when I lost some of my better employees. They went off to become contractors on their own. . . . One reason I have had so much trouble is that I have to keep watching these idiots who are working for me now.
> (Black plumbing contractor, Houston)

Other contractors are currently satisfied with the type of work they are doing but recognize that they could not do other work with their current work force—even if they wanted to. A Mexican-American carpentry contractor doing framing work for residential subdivisions indicated a connection between the relatively low-skilled work he was doing and the skill of the carpenters available to him: "For the quality of work I need, they are OK." He further remarked that the skills of his men were at too low a level for commercial work.

Retention

Each newly established construction firm appears to go through a natural process of sifting to develop a good crew. Contractors hire and lay off constantly as they test candidates for positions with their steady crew of key journeymen whom they keep regularly employed while letting others go with changes in workload. Once a contractor develops what he considers to be a good crew, he does his best to retain them.

Minority contractors who addressed this problem stated that one can keep workers if steady work is available for them. But if a contractor cannot keep a good employee busy continuously, he will lose the worker. Keeping one's work force busy appears to be a major preoccupation of any small contractor with a good crew, and has prompted several contractors to make various efforts to retain their workers. Seven black plumbers in Atlanta, for example, were organized into a loose-knit local chapter of the Eastern Seaboard Plumbers Association, a black plumbers' contracting association headquartered at Hampton Institute in Virginia. The group, in a sense, "pools their work as well as their workers." That is, occasionally if one contractor were short of work, he would call the others until he found one with more upcoming work than he can handle. The inactive contractor would subcontract some of the work from the other plumber, or he would lend employees until work picked up again and he could rehire them. An even more loosely organized group of native Mexican-American contractors in Houston, "Contratistas Mexicanos Unidos," had a similar informal arrangement. In addition, individual contractors occasionally had a standing cooperative arrangement for sharing work and workers with other contractors. Usually, the contractors involved were relatives. In addition to work-sharing arrangements, some contractors lowered prices and even performed work at cost to hold their crews together. Others provided makework or alternative work on properties personally owned by the contractor, or shortened the work week of all employees to allow them to share the work available.

Turnover unrelated to the problem of regularity of work is also a problem for minority contractors. Contractors often lose their good craftsworkers and their better trainees, especially in the nonunion sector. In many cases, the trainees leave because the contractor fails to raise his wage at a rate commensurate with his progress in learning the trade. Consequently, the trainee is attracted to an employer who better appreciates the quality of his newly acquired skills. Of course, the level of compensation is involved in the problem of keeping the highly skilled workers, too. Often the contractors who complain most about turnover also pay the lowest wages.

Training Programs for Employees

Lack of training for employees is cited as a severe problem by only a few contractors. Out of interviews with 282 respondents there were 11 specific mentions of labor training as a critical need for minority contractors. Further, only three out of ten minority firms surveyed participated in any formal training efforts.

If individual minority contractors do not recognize their training needs, several others do. During the course of the interviews in Houston, no fewer than seven proposals for training minority workers by minority contractors were uncovered.

The majority of contractor associations contacted for this study had either a labor training program under way or plans to get one funded and implemented. The NAMC had two successive contracts to promote the National Alliance of Businessmen Job Opportunities in the Business Sector (NAB-JOBS) program, counterparts to contracts awarded to the AGC. Many of these projects have been largely motivated by the lure of available manpower funding; and few have worked very effectively. Further discussion of labor training efforts and the problems associated with them may be found in Chapter 4.

Unquestionably, if minority firms in construction are to grow and advance into larger work, adequate supplies of skilled craftsworkers must be available to them. Of course, the lack of availability of training is related to recruitment problems as well, which is the labor problem most mentioned by minority contractors. As non-union minority firms grow, they will face greater labor-recruitment problems. Further, there was some evidence in the interviews to suggest that union minority contractors have difficulty holding qualified white workers, particularly on ghetto-area projects. Finally, some minority contractors expressed understandable irritation at seeing white firms receive subsidies to train minority workers, when they themselves have been formally or informally training minority workers for years.

Relationships with Unions

As mentioned in previous sections, 49 percent of the contractors had worked under union contract at least part of the time (16 percent in Atlanta; 5 percent in Houston; 74 percent in San Francisco-Oakland; and 65 percent in Chicago). Additionally, some nonunion contractors in the South mentioned that they occasionally used the union referral system for workers. Many others mentioned that they would like to do union work and would contract with a union if they could see the benefit to them.

As a whole, the contractors are not particularly antiunion. Neither are unions foreign institutions to minority contractors. Overall, more than six out of ten had been members of construction unions themselves. Some members still held their union cards and exhibited them with pride. One of the larger black contractors in Atlanta was, in fact, a business agent for the former Masonry Local 9 (a black local) before it was integrated with Masonry Local 8. One of the black contractors in Houston had been a union organizer and union secretary for a Kansas City carpenters' local.

Unions in the mechanical trades show much stronger exclusionary patterns against blacks in the South than in the non-South. Whereas in the non-South nine out of ten former craftworkers in mechanical trades had been union members, only one out of four mechanical-trades craftworkers had been a union member in the South. Most of the black southern mechanical contractors had learned their trades in black colleges, and, upon graduation, went into business for themselves when they could not obtain employment in union construction.

Some contractors, of course, were intensely antiunion, and some contractors had had unfavorable personal experiences with unions. Electrical contractors seemed to have had a greater incidence of such experiences than the others. The only contractors in Atlanta to mention the union as a primary problem was an electrical contractor. In Houston, a black electrical contractor, C. F. Smith, had a well-publicized confrontation with the unions several years ago. Smith says he had sent two of his black employees to join the electrical workers' union but that the local of the IBEW would not admit them. Soon afterward, Smith's firm landed a job in the union sector, and the union picketed the project. Newspapers rose to Smith's defense, challenging the blatant union discrimination tactic of refusing to admit his workers and then refusing to permit him to work because he was nonunion. Years later, Smith still spoke of the experience with some bitterness. [2]

A few contractors are opposed to signing a union contract because of unpleasant personal experiences they had encountered as workers. A black general contractor in Houston recalled the

hostility with which he was greeted in the early 1950s when he
tried to transfer from a carpenters' local in St. Paul, Minnesota,
to an all-white Houston carpenters' local. In fact, he indicated
that this hostility drove him to start his own contracting firm.
Similarly, a Mexican-American air-conditioning contractor de-
clared, "I have been approached several times by the union since
I became an employer; but since they wouldn't let me in as a service employee before, I am not going to join them now."

On the whole, a policy of racial exclusion on the part of a
building-trades local makes little sense and may be a source of
future difficulties. As we have seen, contractors who have experienced discrimination at the hands of unions in the past often have
developed hardened attitudes toward them. Moreover, by refusing
to organize minority contractors, unions violate their own principle
of union security by ignoring a sector of the market.

Largely because of affirmative-action pressures, unions, at
least in Atlanta, have been prodded to act in their own interest.
Herbert Williams, director of the local minority contractor association, noted that on the advent of the Atlanta Plan, union organ-
izers beat a path to the Atlanta Associated Contractors and Trades
Council, Inc. (AAC&TC) office offering to sign up everybody. In
response he observed:

> I don't know what they expect. After so many years of
> keeping us out, now they let the barriers down and
> expect us to jump en masse.
>   They have got to understand that it may not be a
> good thing for all of our contractors to join. There
> has to be something in it for our contractors to gain.
> The decision has to be made on a rational basis. I
> think we will assign a committee to look at their pro-
> posals. [3]

As of 1975, few contractors had signed union contracts. [4]

In neither Houston nor Atlanta were unions strong enough
in residential work to have much influence on minority contractors.
In commercial work, however, the influence of the unions was significant. Reported one nonunion Houston contractor: "You stay away
from certain areas—like downtown." In accord with this statement,
two nonunion minority contractors interviewed complained that
when they bid union work in a traditionally union sector, such as
municipal construction, they would find union firms colluding to
underbid them.

A few of the contractors interviewed had been picketed. A black construction firm in Houston was picketed on a bank remodeling job by a white individual acting on his own behalf. The lone picket upset the bank management so much that although the black firm was permitted to complete the job it had not been invited to bid for further work.

Some minority contractors had suffered significant inconvenience from union actions, but they were usually allowed to complete their work after hours, when union crews were not on the site. One Houston Mexican-American general contractor related that unions stopped his work on a housing project in Galveston in 1959, causing him a loss of $20,000 on the job.

Some contractors encountered less difficulty with unions. One nonunion tile contractor reported that he has no trouble working on union jobs—as long as he pays union scale. In one or two cases, interviews revealed an exceptionally good relationship between unions and minority contractors. One masonry contractor in Atlanta reported that the masonry union has helped him with job referrals.

The majority of southern minority contractors are little affected by unions—mainly because they work in the unorganized residential sector. However, as they grow and expand into commercial work, they will probably follow the pattern of their fellow minority contractors in the non-South and become unionized.

On the whole, the unions in Houston and Atlanta state that they stand ready and willing to organize the minority contractor. Likewise, many of the contractors are agreeable to joining unions if they see the benefit to them. As a black plumbing contractor in Houston stated: "I would rather be union because I would have less trouble in obtaining help. I would join the union if I could see it benefiting me."[5] But there are certain barriers and fears that make the minority contractor reluctant to take such a step.

Most important, minority contractors feared they would not have enough of the better, larger contracts to support union pay rates. With few exceptions, they did not work on this caliber of projects, and several factors inhibited their advancement, leaving them pessimistic about possibilities of working on such projects in the future. If minority contractors continue to do the type of work they have traditionally performed, signing a union contract could be a handicap to them. Even of the few who have signed a contract, a high percentage continued to work nonunion part of the time, especially for the smaller jobs.

Fears of losing control over selection of their work force under union contract bothered many contractors. In the interviews, several contractors pointed out that a union can wreck a contractor by referring inferior workers to him. Many minority contractors had heard of cases in which this has occurred. A well-known illustration is the story of a black electrical contractor in Detroit, who was once a union contractor but left the union after being referred several inferior workers from the union and formed a school to train nonunion minority electrical apprentices. [6]

Interviews revealed that minority contractors believed that only older, less productive, or otherwise inferior workers rely on union referral for work. Since most minority contractors had less steady work than larger white contractors, they were forced to rely on the referral system more than white contractors and thereby had to contend with an inferior work force. In addition, currently many of the unions are all-white, and in the past some white workers refused to work under the supervision of black contractors. Unless the attitudes of these workers change or the racial composition of the unions changes, the contractors feel they would only risk trouble by joining a union.

Fear of losing job control disturbed several contractors. Many contractors expressed concern over losing control of employees under union rules. "You can't even criticize your employees' work without going through a superintendent," says one contractor.

Inability to meet certain provisions of the contract prohibited some contractors from signing union contracts. For example, some union contracts contain the stipulation that a contractor have a field superintendent. But because most minority firms are too small to afford such a position, signing a union contract with such a provision is not realistic.

Some contractors disliked the added burden in office work that unionization brings. Said an Atlanta masonry contractor: "Under the union, I would have to file separate forms for each fringe benefit. . . . With all the extra office requirements, I would have to hire a secretary." He had always performed all the office work himself.

Outside the South, although most of the contractors are union shops, some persist as nonunion firms without encountering opposition from the unions. For example, one nonunion contractor in Chicago, who nonetheless used minority union workers and paid them union scale, said he ran into little resistance from business agents because all his projects were located in black areas where "it isn't safe for whites to work." Further, the business agent does not want to close down the job and throw his men who are making prevailing rates out of a job because he has no replacement jobs for them.

LACK OF MANAGEMENT SKILLS

Lack of management skills was cited by 58 respondents as a primary problem area—the third most often mentioned in the interviews. Further, wherever the subject slipped from the level of individual problems (what are your business problems?) to the group level (what are the problems of minority contractors in general?), contractors often mentioned that what they (the others) needed was better training as managers. Also, many of the larger minority contractors cited lack of business skill as a problem for the small minority contractor.

Typical management and paper work skills essential in construction are estimating and bidding, reading blueprints, bookkeeping, handling finances, managing personnel, and scheduling production. It is easy to see how these needs arise, considering how most subcontractors enter into business. Typically, they come to contracting from a trade in which they are good craftworkers. * Although their technical abilities in the field may be excellent, they usually lack training or experience in business and office-management skills and in technical paper work skills, such as blueprint reading. As noted in the previous chapter, only 20 percent of the contractors had any previous formal business training, and only 31 percent had previous business experience of any kind.

Lack of business experience is often related to other problems, too. Deficiencies in bookkeeping, for example, bear on the contractor's inability to obtain financing and bonding, since a bonding company usually requires that a company have records for the previous three years in good form.

Bookkeeping is one skill that can be fairly easily purchased by hiring a bookkeeper or commissioning an accounting service. In 126 out of 282 cases (or 45 percent) the firm's books are kept by the contractor himself or by immediate family members—in most of these cases, with outside advice and consultation. As Table A.21 illustrates, 158 of 282 contractors employ some form

---

*As the earlier review of backgrounds of contractors interviewed revealed, all subcontractors except those in carpet contracting came to contracting through a trade. The same is usually true of general contractors, who are typically ex-carpenters or ex-masons. However, there are alternative routes to general contracting, such as engineering or construction management. See Table A.5 for a distribution of contractors interviewed by original trade.

of outside help—ranging anywhere from annual assistance with income tax reports to a regular bookkeeping and auditing service
from a firm of certified public accountants.

Other skills are more difficult to obtain. For example, being
able to read and analyze the accounting records—no matter who
keeps them—for cash-flow planning becomes an essential management skill as the firm grows. Similarly, a contractor cannot easily
hire someone to read blueprints; it is difficult to operate without
knowing how to read blueprints for oneself, as the experience of a
Mexican-American painting contractor in Houston bears out. He had
been through one and a half years of apprenticeship school but
dropped out just before the section on reading blueprints. Now he
vitally needs to know this technical skill to figure his bids properly.

Other contractors can be of assistance in providing some
forms of technical assistance to overcome these weaknesses. For
example, one of the electrical contractors interviewed in Atlanta
perfected his estimating techniques with the help of a larger contracting firm. When the black contractor first started bidding
larger jobs, he would submit all of his bids to the other firm's
estimators for checking before turning them in.

One matter that drew some attention in the interviews was
supervision of employees in the field. In the interviews, three or
four contractors mentioned that they encountered supervision problems when they had employees dispersed on different work sites or
when their work forces were large. As one plumbing contractor said,
"You can't trust crews on different sites without a superintendent or
foreman in charge." Two general contractors and one masonry contractor who formerly employed four or five times the number of
workers they currently do mentioned that they have no desire to become that large again—"it is just too much trouble." As one said,
"My blood pressure kicks up to 200 when I have a load of 25 men."

MARKETING

Marketing, or finding jobs, especially plagues contractors
just beginning their businesses. Establishing a construction firm
is not an easy matter—especially if a contractor is from out of
town. With few exceptions, most contractors have to work as employees in the city for many years. Gradually, they learn the local
industry information networks and establish contacts; then they begin on their own. One enterprising interviewee in Houston was able
to shortcut this time-consuming route of experience, however. He
paid a fellow who had "been around the industry a long time" to
accompany him and introduce him to builders.

The problem of finding work is by no means confined to newly established contractors. When asked whether they were getting all the work they could handle, 147 of 279 respondents answered that they were not. The percentage of those who answered that they were working below capacity was dramatically higher outside the South (61 percent) than in the South (36 percent).

Few minority construction firms work exclusively in the minority community. Information from the interviews revealed that Chinese-American contractors worked most in their own community. Black contractors worked less for white (Anglo) customers than did Spanish-American contractors. Several black firms—particularly in Atlanta—directed their marketing pitch at the minority community by advertising in black newspapers and black business directories. Likewise, Chinese-American contractors advertised in Chinese newspapers. Only two Spanish-American contractors reported advertising in Spanish newspapers.

In general, minorities interviewed in the South tended to work less for whites (Anglos) than contractors in the non-South. Whereas five blacks and one Mexican-American in Atlanta and Houston stated they have no white (Anglo) customers whatever, only one Chinese contractor and three Chicago Spanish-American contractors report they have no white (Anglo) customers. Overall, whites (Anglos) make up the smallest proportion of business among black contractors in the South, Spanish-American contractors in Chicago, and Chinese contractors in San Francisco (see Table A.44).

Few contractors reported any difficulty in finding or working for white customers, and no one explicitly termed it a chief problem. One contractor explained that his business was becoming predominantly black because he worked on the western side of metropolitan Atlanta, and he said that whites were moving out of the area to the suburbs.

Subcontractors encounter different problems from general contractors in locating jobs. Often, they faced situations in which the general contractor had chosen his subs in advance or situations where the general contractor had alliances with certain subcontractors which an outsider could not break through, even with a low bid.

The selection of a general contractor is often strongly influenced by the architect. One handicap minority contractors face is the paucity of minority architects to recommend them. In 1971, it was estimated that there were only about 400 licensed black architects in the nation.[7] Field interviews revealed only five licensed black architects in Atlanta and five in Houston.[8] In 1969, only 4 of 400 architects in Houston had Spanish surnames, according to the Roster of Registered Architects published by the Texas Board of

Architectural Engineers.[9] Similarly, a directory of black architects compiled in January 1972 listed only nine black architects in
the San Francisco area.[10]

Architects rarely have any influence over the selection of subcontractors, since the general contractor usually deals directly
with subcontractors. Strong working relationships between white
general contractors and white subcontractors often effectively bar
minority contractors from participating in projects. In fact, a
painting contractor in Houston, interested in breaking into commercial work, contended that if he were able to bid directly to the
owner, he could easily get more jobs.

Almost all of the contractors worked in the city or within
commuting distance of it. The few who did work outside of the
municipal area mentioned that transportation of the crew and travel
expenses are paid by the owner. One poured-terrazzo flooring
contractor in Houston stated that he preferred to work in the rural
areas because he faced less competition there and thus could charge
higher prices.

Part of the minority contractor's inability to find jobs stems
from lack of information on available job opportunities. (See Table
A.45.) Several formal sources of information are available on upcoming construction projects. Perhaps the most respected source,
Dodge Reports, is available in all cities studied on a weekly basis.
In the survey, only 78 contractors of 292 respondents reported that
they use the Dodge Reports (or its sister publication in San Francisco, The Daily Pacific Builder).

In addition to the Dodge Reports, a Builders Exchange exists
in most cities which feeds information on upcoming contracts to its
members and operates a "plans room" for the use of contractors
and subcontractors in estimating. In some cities, information of
contracts awarded and those available for bidding is published in
the AGC News, which is distributed semiweekly to the Houston
chapter membership of the Associated General Contractors (AGC).
The AGC also maintains files of plans on upcoming contracts.
Unfortunately, since most minority contractors are not members
of the Builders Exchange or the AGC, they are excluded from such
information circuits.

Interviews revealed that minorities had little ready access
to information regarding government work in Houston and Atlanta
in 1971. Only 2 minority contractors out of 106 were even on government bid lists. On the other hand, one out of every six interviewees
in 1973-74 in Chicago and San Francisco-Oakland identified government procurement conferences or government bid lists as a source
of information on jobs.

The majority of the minority contractors interviewed do not advertise; and (except in San Francisco), most are not listed in the yellow pages of the telephone book. A few contractors explained that advertisements in newspapers and in the yellow pages tend to draw offers of smaller repair and remodeling jobs—exactly the type of work many of the contractors are trying to avoid. Of course, a few contractors prefer to specialize in small jobs and thus place ads in newspapers (often newspapers directed at the minority community) and solicit work by tacking their business cards on bulletin boards of local grocery stores and laundromats.

In general, minority contractors rely on informal rather than formal sources of information to find jobs. By far the most prevalent source was recommendations from previous customers. Next most often mentioned were minority contractors' associations. Other word-of-mouth referrals come from friends and past associates, fellow contractors who had more work than they could handle, public affirmative-action officers, architects, and even a bonding agent and a union business agent. The heavy reliance on informal sources of information may partly result from most minority contractors' operating in residential markets, which characteristically utilize informal sources. In fact, one contractor mentioned that he relied on informal sources (customer recommendations and callbacks) for residential work but formal sources (Dodge Reports and bid lists) for commercial/industrial work.

Subcontractors aim their marketing efforts toward general contractors. Some subcontractors attempt to introduce themselves to selected builders and general contractors by mail. Others—particularly those whose business is young—will often scout building sites to solicit work. As a firm becomes more established, however, relationships with general contractors are developed and notice of jobs tends to come to the subcontractors without solicitation.

BONDING

Requirements for surety bonding—bid bonds, performance bonds, and payments bonds—exist on virtually all major government contracts and approximately 20 percent of private work. Under the provisions of the Miller Act, contractors on all federal projects over $2,000 are required to be bonded. Similar provisions are in effect for most state and local government contracts across the country.

Surety bonds secure the interests of the project's owner in several ways. Under a performance bond, the surety assumes the owner's financial risks of nonperformance by the contractor. Payment bonds protect the owner against the risk of liens levied by any suppliers the bonded contractor fails to pay.

Inability to obtain surety bonding is popularly identified as a serious—even key—obstacle to the advancement of minority construction firms.[11] Available empirical research on minority contractors indicates that relatively few minority firms have encountered bonding problems. For example, a ten-city survey of minority contractors made by the NAACP in 1970 concluded:

> Many firms replied they had no problems in securing performance bonds, but this may be explained partly by the fact that few firms did much government work on projects large enough to require bonding, and therefore have never even tried to secure it. To the simple question of whether or not they had trouble in securing bonds, most firms answered in the negative, but this may be because few had ever tried. <u>This survey did not conclusively show bonding as a prime deterrent to participation by minority firms in major government work.</u> But the results certainly do not disprove this long-believed notion. Instead they illustrate how complex the problem really is.[12] [Emphasis added]

A more thorough study by Theresa Shapiro, which surveyed black contractors in New Orleans, found only 7 contractors out of 184 (or 4 percent) who cited "securing a performance bond" as their single greatest problem.[13] Further, 63 percent of the 184 contractors interviewed had never even sought or received a performance bond. Similarly, in the present study, only 23 contractors out of 282 ranked bonding among their three top problems.

How can we account for the apparent discrepancy between conventional wisdom and empirical evidence? Of course, part of the answer is simply that few minority contractors have advanced to the point where they require bonding. Of 296 respondents in this study, 124 contractors (or 42 percent) had never applied for bonding. Most said they had not done so because they had never needed it.

Examination of the characteristics of the contractors who do rate bonding as a chief problem casts light on the nature of the problem. Bonding appears to be a requirement more commonly affecting the general contractor than the specialty contractor. In Shapiro's study, six of the seven contractors who cited "securing a performance bond" as their single greatest problem were general contractors.[14] In this present study, 18 out of 32 respondents who termed bonding a chief problem were general contractors. Bonds may be required of subcontractors, but more often subcontractors work under the bond of the general contractor.

Second, bonding appears to be a problem affecting the larger contractor. Of those who described bonding as a chief problem, 80 percent had a gross dollar volume of $50,000 or more. This conclusion was borne out in various statements by minority contractors during the interviews. When asked whether they had ever attempted to obtain bonding, many of the contractors answered no, then added, "I am not into that big work."

Third, bonding is a discontinuous sort of a problem, primarily affecting contractors seeking their first bond or attempting to obtain their initial bond at a higher bonding level. For example, one Chinese-American general contractor ran into bonding problems when he attempted to undertake a $4 million project after having performed on $400,000 jobs. One Atlanta contractor expressed the point another way, "We are okay for bonding and financing as long as we don't do any project over $300,000." All of this, of course, means that bonding will assume greater importance as minority contractors advance into the mainstream of construction work.

That nine out of ten of the contractors do not rate bonding as one of their chief problems does not mean bonding has little effect on minority firms. In answer to the question: "Has bonding kept you off work you would like to do?" 46 of 134 contractors (or 34 percent) in the Chicago and the San Francisco areas answered affirmatively.

Fourth, the interviews revealed that some minority contractors who reported difficulty obtaining bonding were not qualified. However, the bonding problems of a few minority contractors were due to discrimination, which may take various forms.

The Runaround

According to this discriminatory tactic, the contractor's application package never seems to be complete. When the contractor provides all of the information, the agent tells him that he needs additional information. When the contractor returns to provide the extra document, he is met with still further requests, and so forth. This game goes on sometimes until past the bid deadline or until the contractor simply gives up any idea of trying to obtain a bond. This tactic is usually aimed at minority contractors who have not been previously bonded and who do not understand bonding procedures.

The Double Standard

Because bonding standards are subjective, an agent can apply tougher standards to a minority contractor than to an identically qualified white contractor. For example, interviewees cited cases in which minority contractors were required to have greater "net quick" or greater liquid assets than their white counterparts. Of course, this sort of discrimination is difficult to prove.

That minority contractors consider the double standard a prevalent practice is important in itself. Further, the negative image of surety practices is only reinforced by the apparently common practice of agents' refusing to disclose reasons for denying a bond. Such secrecy only intensifies the suspicions of those predisposed to anticipate discrimination anyway.

Higher Charges

Some companies bond minority contractors only at rates substantially above the market level.

In addition to personal bigotry on the part of a few individual agents, there are elements of institutional discrimination involved in the bonding problem. Lack of equal access to financing, inferior educational background and job experience, lack of familiarity with procedures used by the insurance industry—all are relevant factors woven into the fabric of our society.

The problem is further complicated by another institutional factor: in candid discussion, surety officials admit that bonding agencies and companies are reluctant to bond any small company—especially on an initial bond, because the commissions and profits sometimes do not cover all of the administrative expenses of processing a contractor's application for a bond. Thus, at least part of the bonding problems of minority contractors can be attributed to their size rather than their minority status.

Finally, the bonding problem is an inflamed issue for some minorities on ideological grounds. According to this argument, the surety industry is considered to have a public trust—a special responsibility, since it is publicly licensed (by the U.S. Department of Treasury) and because it is largely supported by government-imposed bonding requirements. Yet it is a "lily-white" industry. As of June 1974, not a single minority-owned surety company accredited by the U.S. Department of the Treasury existed nor were there more than a handful of minority surety agents in the entire country. Further, this industry, with its powers to screen out contractors from performing government work, stands in the way of using government procurement as an instrument to upgrade minority contractors, providing them with a track record on larger projects

CHEAPER COMPETITION

Cheaper competition was regarded as a major problem by[25] contractors surveyed. Many worked in trades with easy entry requirements, such as tile or painting, and faced competition on residential work from smaller "scabs" (nonunion contractors) and "illegals" (contractors operating without a license or business registration). Contractors in strictly licensed trades such as plumbing or electrical work were protected from the latter problem. Other contractors were troubled by another form of fierce competition: a market dominated by larger established firms that could purchase materials more cheaply.

The San Francisco area was the origin of most of the complaints about cheap competition. Many of these came from union painting firms specializing in residential work. Four painting contractors indicated they found it difficult to compete with nonunion contractors who operate without a license. A few other specialty contractors also complained about "scab" competition. Nonunion competition has an especially adverse impact on Chinese union contractors operating in Chinatown; many Chinese firms are not under union agreements and pay considerably less than union wage rates.

Some San Francisco contractors also complained about particularly fierce competition from larger rivals. For example, two ironwork contractors who purchased their steel from larger combination contractor-wholesale houses appeared to be at the mercy of these suppliers. By controlling the price and availability of steel, the suppliers allegedly skimmed off all the better jobs for themselves, leaving only undesirable smaller jobs for the minority contractors interviewed. Other contractors in various trades voiced complaints about having to compete with "large established firms—with dependable employees and buying power." In Chicago, a contractor who owned a relatively new steel-fabrication firm and was attempting to break into the market for larger jobs competing directly with very large firms, stated: "This is just a difficult field to break into. The firms in the business in this area are very well established and have been around a long time."

Six contractors in Houston termed cheap competition as their primary problem. Of these six, five were tile contractors. The other contractor was a linoleum layer who contracts his own labor only. The nonunion tile sector in Houston appeared to operate on an extremely competitive basis. At least two contractors referred to such corrupt practices as kickbacks and bid peddling as being fairly common in the industry. A couple of others were concerned about tile wholesalers' operating contracting firms themselves. Interviewees also cited the problem of wholesalers selling to general contractors, leaving the tile contractors to supply labor only (thus losing money by missing the opportunity to provide materials). The tile industry in Houston was also highly competitive because it was a center of employment for illegal labor from Mexico who worked for wages below the federal minimum, according to several contractors.

Two contractors in Atlanta complained of cheap competition. One, a masonry contractor, complained of what he called "backyard competition" by brick masons who operate as contractors without carrying insurance or paying sales taxes, social security, or any other payroll tax. He said it was difficult to remain in the business as a licensed contractor, obeying all the provisions of the law, while competing with contractors with such illegal lower operating costs. The other contractor, a dry-wall contractor, similarly complained about this illegal cheap competition as well as competition from the larger firms, who are able to purchase materials at quantity discounts—sometimes directly from the factory or source. The problem of competing against those who can obtain quantity discounts was cited by a couple of small plumbing contractors in Houston, too. Many of the smaller contractors have access to supplies only at retail prices with a contractors' discount rather than at wholesale rates.

Perhaps there is a difficult middle position—small enough to be doing less desirable work and to be bothered by small firms using illegal practices but large enough to be underbid on better jobs by the larger firms. Unfortunately, several minority contractors interviewed fell into this position.

COLLECTION

Overall, 21 of the 282 contractors stated that their major problem was collection—either from customers or general contractors. For marginal contractors—especially those who can exercise little choice in the matter of selection of customers—collecting is a major problem indeed. Collection problems were also more common with specialty contractors who performed work near the completion of the job, such as tile or air-conditioning contractors. One Mexican-American air-conditioning contractor in Houston sadly related that he had had to foreclose on the biggest job of his career—an $8,100 air-conditioning installation project on a church. His court case was successful, and he obtained possession of the structure. "But," he shrugged, "what can I do with a church?"

Some of the subcontractors are in a better marketing position so that they can afford to "pick and choose" for whom they work. Such subcontractors reported using a variety of methods of checking out a builder or general contractor, including the following:
(1) checking with the contractor's supplier to see if he pays for his

materials on time; (2) asking other subcontractors if the contractor
paid them on time; (3) consulting the Better Business Bureau;
(4) checking his Dun and Bradstreet rating, if he is rated; and
(5) checking with a subcontractors' association for the sort of reputation the general contractor has with them.

Most contractors classify collection problems as day-to-day
difficulties rather than obstacles inhibiting the firm's expansion.
But if the unpaid debts are large or if the missed payments occur at
a critical time, they can stop a contractor from taking on new work
or they can even drive one out of business.

OBTAINING LICENSES

Inability to obtain licensing is popularly cited as a severe
problem for minority contractors. For example, a recent study
by the Educational Testing Service described in some detail the
licensing problems encountered by a black plumber in Montgomery
County, Alabama. [15] The study further explained that the problem
of minority participation in construction generally is primarily one
of access to training, and only secondly one of securing licenses. [16]
Interviews for the present study provide some additional perspective
on the issue of licensing minority contractors.

Licensing in construction is performed by local governments,
by the state, or by both. Licenses are generally required only in
selected trades (usually electrical, plumbing, and air conditioning-
heating, and sometimes general contractors). An exception to this
statement is California, where contractors in every trade are
licensed by the state.

Inability to obtain licensing was a problem for minority contractors only in certain areas. Only one contractor among the 315
interviewed—an electrical contractor in Chicago—mentioned that
licensing was a severe problem. At least three electrical contractors interviewed in that city independently indicated that a bribe of
$20,000 was required to obtain an electrical contractor's license.
The contractors added that such a bribe was required of applicants
regardless of race or ethnic background. The author was unable to
verify whether such "under-the-table" money was indeed required;
but the assertion was widely believed among the contractors interviewed and merits an investigation at least to dispel a widely held
notion.

During the course of collecting information from experts outside the project cities, other problems connected with licensing
were uncovered. One fellow complained that in Alabama it is difficult for a black to obtain a state general contractor's license; and

without it, general contractors are limited to jobs of $20,000 and under. The interviewee indicated he knew of not a single state-licensed black contractor in Alabama in mid-1973. He was attempting to obtain a state license and had completed his application except for a required letter of recommendation from an existing state-licensed general contractor. The interviewee indicated that he did not know any white contractor in Alabama well enough to ask for such a recommendation.

Another problem associated with licensing occasionally occurred with Spanish-speaking contractors and journeymen where tests were given only in English. For example, Latin Builders Association, an organization of Cuban contractors, had been concerned with the fact that journeymen and contractor licensing exams in Miami were given only in English. After a lengthy struggle, the Cuban contractors were forced to pay others to "master" for them, that is, to sign the building permit but not to be involved in the actual construction. Language barriers in licensing journeymen also artificially created a labor shortage situation for Cuban firms, although the contractors claimed that qualified Cuban workers were available. [17] The Latin contractors, whose influence was considerable since they account for an estimated 40 percent of all construction put in place in Dade County, [18] have prevailed in their struggle with local authorities, so that by 1974, examinations were offered in Spanish. [19]

The California state contractor's licensing system received favorable reviews from those interviewed. Even contractors who indicated that they had to take the exams more than once to pass it did not complain that licensing was unjust; in fact, several praised the system for its fairness. Since California has the most extensive licensing system of any area covered in the study, it appears that licensing can be well administered so as not to act as a bar to minority participation in construction.

DISCRIMINATION

In the South, only two contractors identified overt acts of discrimination as problems. One, a black general contractor, alleged that a city inspector had discriminated against him. The other, a black electrical contractor, stated that "up until last year, my biggest problem was discrimination by the union."

It appears that blatant acts of discrimination have been reduced considerably. This is not to say that overt acts of discrimination no longer occur, just that they are less common and are less likely to inhibit the contractor from advancing. Several contractors stated that the environment was improving. Some of the older contractors lamented that they wished they could be beginning their careers now because the opportunities look better than they ever have. Many related experiences of blatant discrimination in the past. For example, one black masonry contractor noted that there once was a time when black contractors could not subscribe to the Atlanta Daily Builders Report (a listing of projects up for bid and projects for which a building permit has been issued). He recalls: "When you walked into a white contractor's office and a copy of it was sitting on his desk, he would cover it over, as if you were not supposed to know it existed."

A Mexican-American terrazzo contractor in Houston claimed that when he went into business in 1964, he was unable to purchase any equipment in Houston for pouring terrazzo. Suppliers had been forbidden by the Terrazzo and Stone Association to sell such equipment to outsiders; consequently, the contractor had to order the machinery directly from Minneapolis.

Practically every illustration of overt discrimination against the contractors related in the interviews referred to experiences of several years ago. Today discrimination shows up in a more elusive and insidious form—covert discrimination. For example, Sultan Ghani, a black Atlanta painting contractor, recently submitted the low bid on three painting contracts with the Atlanta public school system. Ghani alleges that he was denied the contract because he had failed to check a certain appropriate box signifying that he had seen the addenda to the blueprints—even though it was clear and obvious from a look at his bids that he had taken them into account. It is easy for one unfamiliar with paper work to be trapped on such a technicality. When a contractor has been out of the mainstream, procedures within the mainstream are new and unfamiliar, and strict enforcement can keep him out. Another black painting contractor interviewed has since performed work for the public school system, but he did so under the name of a white contracting firm.

There are other examples of what being out of the mainstream means. Most minority contractors are subs, and most white (Anglo) general contractors already have a group of favorite subcontractors with whom they have become accustomed to working. As a subcontractor in Houston said, the only way a black contractor can break in is to underbid greatly, thus cutting his own profit. Further, the 80 percent of the black contractors who do not hold memberships in white contractors' associations are excluded from important information networks.

Lack of information is often part of the problem. For example, the minority contractor who has been out of the mainstream may not know the proper form in which to put his financial records for examination by bonding companies. He may not be receiving information on jobs because he is outside contractors' associations and other important informal networks in the construction industry. For example, city agencies fail to send him a letter announcing a new project because they do not know he is in business.

Although only one or two contractors labeled racial discrimination by unions as a chief problem, other minority contractors referred to it in the interviews. The two issues that received the most attention were getting their men into the union and obtaining incompetent referrals. The latter problem is usually not solely one of racial discrimination, but occasionally discrimination does enter into the picture.

Contractors also face discrimination in finding customers. There are "white jobs" and "black jobs." For example, servicing air conditioners can be a "black job," but few whites would allow blacks to install one (traditionally a "white job"). This is so even though servicing an air conditioner in some cases may require more skill than installing one. Blacks appear to get traditional black jobs more easily than traditional white jobs. For instance, in Houston, one contractor's service business runs 90 percent white, but his installation business is only 5 percent white.

Eight complaints of racial discrimination as a chief problem came from the San Francisco-Oakland area. Of these, one was a very specific charge, filed with the Equal Employment Opportunity Commission (EEOC), against the glaziers union, for refusing entry, and six others failed to mention any details. However, four noted problems in obtaining white customers later in the interview. In fact, overall a quarter of the contractors interviewed in San Francisco and Chicago acknowledged that they had difficulty obtaining white (Anglo) customers. The strongest evidence of such difficulty was among Chinese-American contractors and the weakest was among Japanese and Spanish-American contractors—all in San Francisco. Further insight on this issue came in interviews with white contractors. One, a foreigner from Rumania, complained that he faced discrimination in finding customers. Another, an Irish specialty contractor, when asked how he found general contractors to work for, said spontaneously: "They find me. They're all Irish!"

Discrimination against minorities is not confined to the white community. When asked why he failed to use the only black building-supply house in Atlanta, one black contractor answered in a sincere and serious tone: "Well, you know, when it comes to financial matters, you just can't trust a Negro." Several black subcontractors in Oakland and Chicago complained bitterly about particular black general contractors who avoid using black subs.

In summary, there has been a reduction in overt discrimination. Yet covert discrimination—forms of discrimination that do not stop at the edge of the white community but actually permeate the self-image of the black community too—have yet to be eliminated.

Interviews in late 1973 and early 1974 indicated that the problems of inflation and shortages were drawing increasing attention from minority contractors. Whereas not a single firm mentioned inflation as a problem in Houston and Atlanta in 1971, 12 minority contractors in Chicago and San Francisco-Oakland rated it as one of their chief problems.

Small firms are hit hard by inflation of building material prices. Unable to stockpile, they are at the mercy of the market. Bids made at low material prices often have to be made good, even at sacrifice of profit. Facing unstable supply markets, contractors chafe at any long delays between bid deadlines and groundbreaking, as are often involved in government work. A few contractors mentioned that they avoid government work for this reason.

The problems presented small contractors by inflation are often compounded by the measures taken to remedy it. Small contractors are among the hardest hit by rising interest rates. With meager equity resources, such businesses must rely on borrowed funds to undertake any sizable jobs.

CONCLUSIONS

Minority contractors and subcontractors face a multitude of problems in expanding their businesses. They are beset by all the difficulties faced by small entrepreneurs, compounded by all the problems associated with minority status. The two problem areas most often mentioned by the contractors interviewed were lack of financing, particularly interim financing, and difficulties in finding and keeping capable workers. Other major problems were lack of management skills, inability to obtain workers, bonding, debt collection (especially for smaller contractors), inability to obtain jobs (in Houston), and price competition, discrimination, and inflation.

The problems of minority contractors can usefully be viewed as a stream. Problems are omnipresent throughout the life of the minority firms, but the composition of the problems changes with the stage of a firm's development. The cross-section of the stream, representing the mix of problems a contractor faces at any given time, is determined by several factors, including length of time in business, volume of work, size of contracts performed, and type of construction (for example, service/rehabilitation/repair or new work; residential or commercial/industrial work). The width of the stream at any point provides a rough indication of the dimensions of problems a firm faces. Problems are greatest in the beginning and in the more advanced stages (such as larger commercial work). Through any part of the stream, one could take a "slice," which would represent a mix of problems present in that stage of the firm's development.

Of course, the problems vary by trade. For example, a sheet-metal contractor faces a higher financial-entry threshold to establish his firm than does a tile contractor. Similarly, a general contractor is more likely to encounter bonding problems than would a specialty contractor. Problems differ according to trade because many significant differences exist among the trades—differences in the mode of operation; differences in the operating capital required (which varies according to such factors as what stage of building the contractor works on, how fast he completes his job, or how long between roughing and finish); differences in capital equipment required (which varies according to the type of project and the nature of the trade); differences in the licensing provisions or lack of same for the trade; and differences in the degree of competition in the trade.

The characteristics of a problem often change as the firm moves through the various stages of development. For example, whereas lack of management skills in the early stages comprises such matters as bookkeeping, in the later stages it refers to more complex tasks such as production scheduling or cash-flow management. However, the problem of lack of management skills declines at some point because certain specialized management talent can be purchased outside the firm. Thus, the survey located a contractor with a third-grade education managing a multimillion dollar enterprise with a staff that included personnel with master's degrees in business. In many trades, certain problems intensify as the contractor moves from one type of work to another (from remodel work to new work, or from residential work to commercial work). In other trades, they may diminish as the stage of development advances.

Placed within the framework of the "problem stream," the problems encountered by the minority contractor in a given trade fall into patterns. Financing is generally a problem throughout all stages of development, although it is a crucial entry obstacle in certain trades, such as ironwork or sheet-metal contracting. Labor, on the other hand, does not become a problem until the firm has some employees. As a minority contractor's firm grows and hires a work force, the contractor attempts to sift through the workers hired, selecting the better workers to remain with the firm permanently as a "steady crew" or "key personnel." However, to maintain a steady crew intact, the firm must be able to keep them busy. Thus, the contractor becomes more concerned with marketing and maintaining a constant or increasing volume of business. As the firm grows, its need for skilled personnel increases, as does the contractor's concern for recruiting and training. As a firm grows larger still, achieves a more stable level of work, and becomes unionized, the contractor's labor recruitment and training problems diminish because he can rely on union referral to obtain workers. His chief personnel worries may then focus on recruiting a competent supervisory staff. A problem affecting only the larger contractor is bonding. Both financing and bonding intensify in discontinuous leaps or "bumps" as the firm grows or the contractor breaks into a new type of work. For example, when a contractor begins performing commercial work, his financial problems are increased because commercial work is more commonly contracted on a 10 percent retainage basis than is residential construction.

Certain problems are a greater burden on small or new contractors than they are on those who have reached large or medium size. For example, finding jobs is likely to be a problem affecting recent entrants into the business or into a particular stage of the business (such as commercial work). Debt collection appears to have the greatest impact on small marginal contractors—especially those who can exercise little choice as to customers. Likewise, competition appears to hurt the smaller firm most, since it faces competition from craftsworkers who operate illegally as subcontractors on small jobs without carrying insurance, or paying sales taxes, social security, or other payroll taxes. Cheaper competition characteristically is a problem for contractors in trades with easy entry requirements, such as tiling or residential painting. Contractors in strictly licensed trades, such as plumbing or electrical work, are protected from this problem. As a firm grows, competition comes from larger contractors who can obtain their building materials more cheaply. Many of the smaller firms that are only able to buy supplies at discounted retail prices have to compete against larger firms that have access to supplies at wholesale rates.

Of course, certain problems are aggravated by recession and high interest rates. These include financing, reported to be the worst problem even in relatively prosperous times, and competing for scarce materials in shortage situations. Facing such problems, the small contractor has few resources and little power to cope.

The survey of minority contractors, which reflected a sample biased to include a greater than proportionate mix of larger firms, showed a definite pattern. A scattering of contractors mentioned problems characteristic of small or new firms. Many more respondents indicated encountering labor and financial problems. Only a few had faced the bonding problem, which receives the most attention from the press.

In summary, minority contractors face the problems of being small, compounded by problems of their minority status. For example, although almost all contractors face problems of financing, minorities generally have had fewer internal resources and external contacts to draw upon, Similarly, though most small contractors are adversely affected by the recession, those minority contractors who work proportionately more in the minority community are more hurt as their traditional customers are harder hit.

Regardless of trade or stage of development, problems are so omnipresent that most minority contractors do not consider the future beyond the logistics of meeting the next Friday's payroll. Many work so hard—supervising, estimating, working at the trade with the crew, hunting personnel or finances, bookkeeping—that they have little time to plan for upgrading. They conduct all of the firm's business by themselves and live day to day or week to week, concentrating on merely surviving. When they do turn their attention to the future for a moment, they express varied plans and ambitions, reflecting the diversity of their situations.

NOTES

1. Personal interview with Mario Quinones, member of steering committee to organize the Pan American Bank, Houston, September 19, 1971.

2. Personal interview with C. F. Smith, electrical contractor, Houston, May 28, 1971.

3. Personal interview with Herbert Williams, executive director, AAC&TC, Atlanta, April 16, 1975.

4. Telephone interview with Herbert Williams, April 16, 1975.

5. Personal interview with Alvin Herbert, black plumbing contractor, Houston, April 18, 1971.

6. Personal interview with C. F. Smith.

7. "Architecture's New Wave, " Ebony, June 1971, pp. 33-42.

8. Interviews with John S. Chase, first black licensed architect in the state of Texas, Houston, April 19, 1971, and with Herbert Williams, May 13, 1971.

9. Cited in Francis Scott Yeager "Economic Report Prepared for the Steering Committee of the Proposed Pan American National Bank" (Houston, Texas, May 15, 1969), mimeographed, p. 22.

10. San Francisco Redevelopment Agency, "Black Architects and Engineers in the West," 1972, mimeographed.

11. For example, see Burt Schorr, "Black Construction Contractors Find Selves Cut Out of Lucrative Long-Term Contracts,"
Wall Street Journal, May 7, 1971: Reginald Stuart, Black Contractors' Dilemma (Nashville, Tenn.: Race Relations Information Center, 1971), p. 22; G. Douglas Pugh, "Bonding Minority Contractors," in Black Economic Development ed. William F. Haddad and
G. Douglas Pugh (Englewood Cliffs, N.J.: Prentice-Hall,
1969) pp. 138-50; and Joseph Debro, "The Minority Builder,"
Labor Law Journal 21 (May 1970): 298-309.

12. U.S. Department of Housing and Urban Development,
Office of the Assistant Secretary of Equal Opportunity, A Survey of
Minority Construction Contractors (Washington, D.C.: Government
Printing Office, 1971), p. 31.

13. Theresa R. Shapiro, Black Construction Contractors in
New Orleans (New Orleans: Division of Business and Economic Research, Louisiana State University, undated), Research Study No.
14, p. 23.

14. Ibid.

15. Benjamin Shimberg, Barbara F. Esser, and Daniel H.
Kruger, Occupational Licensing: Practices and Policies (Washington, D.C.: Public Affairs Press, 1972).

16. Ibid.

17. William S. Franklin, "Cuban Contractors in Miami and
Dade County, Florida," paper presented at the Southern Economic
Association annual convention, November 1973, Houston. Data
apply to the 1971 calendar year.

18. Ibid.

19. Telephone interview with Augustine Alvarez, director,
Latin Builders Association, Miami, Florida, February 24, 1974.

4

APPROACHES TO UPGRADING THE MINORITY CONTRACTOR: DEMAND STIMULATION AND SUPPLY DEVELOPMENT

The remainder of this book deals with approaches to upgrading minority construction contractors. Efforts to assist minority contractors can be roughly divided into two classifications: those that concentrate on stimulating demand for the product or services of minority firms (procurement or job-development efforts) and those that attempt to enhance the capacity of the minority firm to do larger or more work (bonding assistance, financial assistance, technical and managerial assistance, and labor training). Individual approaches to demand stimulation and supply development are considered. In the following two chapters, two vehicles that seem to combine both approaches—the joint venture and the minority contractor association—are examined.

THE DEMAND-STIMULATION APPROACH

The basic objective of the demand-stimulation approach is to increase the volume of work contracted to minority firms. The approach is built upon the assumption that capabilities to perform the work exist currently among minority firms or can relatively easily be developed through on-the-job experience. Demand stimulation involves the redirection of procurement policies to increase the volume of construction work performed by minority contractors. Attempts have been made to redirect both private and public procurement through publication of lists identifying minority contractors. However, since public procurement and procurement by government contractors is more subject to policy manipulation, they receive most of the effort.

Some writers have suggested that government expenditures, which make up such a large portion of total construction expenditures, can fruitfully be directed to assist minority contractors. Several government programs have been based in part on this rationale. In support of this view, Debro argues: "Construction in the public sector represents the greatest opportunity for minority builders since there exists the legal requirement of open, competitive bids."[1]

On the other hand, Mills points out that precisely because competitive bidding is required on publicly assisted jobs, and the lowest responsible bidder must be selected, "opportunities for favoring minority contractors [on public jobs] are limited" and thus "the greatest promise of assistance to black contractors is through cooperation with larger contractors on private financed jobs." Mills argues that private work offers more flexibility to assist minority contractors.[2]

In fact, however, competitive bidding is not required on all public construction. For example, the New York State Urban Development Corporation (UDC) negotiates its contracts bypassing the policy of accepting the lowest bidder.[3] As one consequence of this negotiation procedure, minority firms in New York State received more than $124 million in contracts from 1971 through June 30, 1974, either as exclusive contractors or through joint ventures with larger white contractors.[4]

Remarks made by contractors interviewed regarding government work provide further indication that competive bidding is not always prevalent. Several respondents indicated that despite open-bidding requirements, in practice obtaining government contracts is a highly political matter. It was the view of some contractors that "one has to be politically connected in order to obtain the larger government contracts."

The issue of bidding requirements aside, it is perhaps most useful to view government construction as a form of work possessing certain advantages as well as disadvantages. On the one hand, a contractor can build his business through public work. An established white contractor indicated that he had built up his business initially by performing government work, which he termed "one of the few available routes to breaking into construction." Since becoming established, however, he performed mainly private work.

On the other hand, public work is regarded as exceptionally difficult because much of it has several undesirable characteristics: abundance of paper work, bonding requirements, payment lags, inspection requirements, greater vulnerability to sudden changes in public policy (such as the 18-month moratorium on housing projects imposed in 1973). In addition, certain types of government work are subject to fierce competition and thus low profit margins. For example, according to several persons interviewed, when work slows, many larger white contractors will bid on government housing projects at break-even or a very small margin to keep their established crews busy and intact while waiting for more lucrative jobs in the private market. As another example, the FHA repossessed-housing program in some places has the reputation among minority contractors of being cutthroat and undesirable. As one black contractor in Houston describes it: "This is the sort of work which keeps us poor." Even in heavily unionized areas, FHA repossessed-housing work is generally nonunion because it comes under the $2,000 limit to which the Davis-Bacon Act of 1931 applies. According to Davis-Bacon provisions, prevailing wage rates must be paid on work performed under federal government contract. Since much of FHA repossessed housing work is excluded from coverage by Davis-Bacon, contractors, free to compete for such work by undercutting labor standards, often do so. Thereby, they squeeze out of the market contractors who pay prevailing wages.

Bidding and contracting procedures are so formidable in some agency work that some contractors, having invested so much in learning the procedures, may attempt to specialize in the business. However, market specialization in construction may be dangerous. Facing the insecurity inherent in unstable construction markets, the wise contractor attempts to diversify his business as much as possible.

In conclusion, a newly established contractor cannot afford to ignore any market sector. If the firm is to grow, it cannot be limited to private work exclusively or for that matter to government work. As a contractor grows and becomes more established, he becomes more selective as to the type of work he will accept. Some wish to concentrate on government projects, while others will not touch them.

Interestingly, although government procurement offers promise in assisting growing minority contractors, no affirmative-action requirements for utilizing minority enterprise have been implemented as counterpart to the affirmative-action requirements for minority employment specified in Executive Order 11246. However, a variety of scattered efforts to promote participation of minority contractors in public construction work have been undertaken over the past decade. In the following sections, these efforts are examined and reviewed as to their effectiveness.

Identifying Minority Firms

One of the chief forms of efforts to upgrade minority contractors to date is identifying minority firms in construction. The U.S. Department of Housing and Urban Development (HUD) alone has spent more than three quarters of a million dollars for this purpose. This approach is based on the assumption that a major deterrent to affirmative action to increase participation of minority firms on federal work has been a lack of knowledge as to the identity of minority-group construction contractors.

Because construction firms are generally less visible than other types of business enterprise, efforts at identification may not be unreasonable. As noted in Chapter 2, the majority of minority contractors generally do not have offices but rather operate out of their homes. Further, since few minority contractors are listed in the telephone book and fewer than one out of four belong to a nonminority trade association, they are difficut to locate.

The most extensive attempts to identify minority contractors nationally have been the efforts funded by HUD. In July 1969, HUD issued a $173,760 contract to the NAACP to compile a survey of minority contractors in the United States to be used in matching minority firms with contract opportunities on federal or federally assisted projects. The NAACP in turn subcontracted the task of identifying Spanish-surnamed contractors to Jobs for Progress, Inc., Operation Service, Employment and Redevelopment (SER). The findings of this 48-city survey were published as a six-volume Registry of Minority Construction Contractors in July 1970. The registry contains more addresses, and some background information on 2,051 black and Spanish-surnamed contractors.

In spring 1972, HUD awarded $391,000 to the National Urban League Development Foundation and $191,000 to SER to update and expand the listing to include all minority professionals involved in housing production or urban development in 89 cities across the nation. SER subcontracted its work on the project to Juarez and Associates, a consulting firm owned by a former executive director of SER.[5]

Information was collected from March through May of 1972, compiled, and submitted to HUD in September. A year later, HUD published the results of the survey in a ten-volume Registry of Minority Contractors and Housing Professionals.

In August 1974, a $52,020 contract was awarded to a private firm—Ken Guscott Associates of Boston—to provide a second update of the Registry.

In addition to the HUD efforts, a wide variety of public agencies and private organizations publish listings of minority businesses, including construction contractors. A geographically arranged compilation of such listings has been published each September by the National Minority Business Campaign.[6] This listing is by no means complete, but it is the best regularly published compilation.

Compiling lists of minority contractors has inherent limitations, namely:

1. Lists provide a static picture of a dynamic market situation. Any published listing quickly becomes out of date. Such obsolescence occurs so rapidly that a delay of any significant length between collection and publication of information means that the list is significantly inaccurate even upon publication.

2. A mere listing of names and addresses and phone numbers with no reference to the specialty and capability may do more harm than good. For example, persons interviewed cited several cases of white contractors or customers trying one name on a list, finding the contractor unsuitable, and, soured by the experience, giving up the idea of utilizing minority contractors.

3. When descriptive information on minority firms is provided, it is often more suitable to manufacturing businesses than construction. For example, one of the most detailed listings of minority contractors in the San Francisco area is published by a private firm, Source Publications in Berkeley. In this publication, every firm is listed with a full-page description. Unfortunately, many of the characteristics detailed—such as square feet of available storage space, quality control, pieces/rates—are inappropriate to construction, while critical information such as union status, bonding capacity, and license number are omitted. The Source Publications listing is not atypical in this regard. The HUD Registry of Minority Contractors and Housing Professionals listed all contractors together in one category, failing to specify specialties.

4. Even if complete and accurate, lists will not ensure greater utilization of minority contractors. Lists by themselves do not generate jobs for minority contractors; they can only provide general contractors and construction owners with knowledge of contractors. Indeed, this knowledge can be misused, harming the minority. For example, a white general contractor can request a bid from a listed minority without ever intending to accept it. In this case, the minority takes the time and expense to prepare a bid for no possibility of return. A few contractors interviewed had had such experiences leaving them embittered and generally distrustful of bid requests from unfamiliar sources.

This does not mean that listings are useless or unnecessary. An up-to-date list of capable minority contractors is a fine tool in the hands of a vigorous compliance officer or minority contractor association. One of the best examples of an effectively used list is one published by the affirmative-action office of the San Francisco Redevelopment Agency (SFRA). Originated in 1967, the list has been updated several times. The SFRA list includes only firms with state licenses and is conveniently arranged by trade. However, its chief limitation is that it provides no indication of the capabilities of individual firms so that, for example, under the category "iron-work" are listed businesses that specialize in ornamental ironwork, reinforcing ironwork, fence building, and tool sharpening.

Such a limitation would be severe in the absence of someone with fuller knowledge to match firms with opportunities. On the basis of the information listed as well as his personal knowledge of the capabilities of individual contractors, the agency's affirmative-action officer, Benson Hattem, individually recommends minority contractors and nonminority contractors to one another. Further, he generally follows up to find if the match was successful. Several minority contractors interviewed observed that Hattem had been of "as much or greater assistance" to them in securing work than were the efforts of any of the minority contractor associations to which they belonged.

While generating lists of minority contractors is by itself of questionable usefulness, identification of minority firms is a necessary part of any effective effort to upgrade them. Thus, guidelines for compiling listings are provided in the following paragraphs.

First, listings are best generated locally and continually updated. Second, each list should be dated according to when the information was collected, so that users can evaluate the obsolescence factor. Third, listings are most useful if organized by trade—preferably with some information noting the capacity and specialities (if any) of each contractor. Fourth, in order to locate as complete a listing of contractors as possible, it is essential to utilize a wide variety of information resources. * Probably the most fertile source of information is referral from the contractors themselves. Contractors can make referrals to firms that would not otherwise be found. In view of this, minority contractor associations are natural vehicles for collection of such information. Many contractor

---

*For a description of sources employed in this study, see Table A.45.

associations collect such information anyway as part of their regular functions. Under past practices, they have been a major supplier of information to others who in turn get paid for it. Further,
associations know the construction industry better than do local
chapters of civil rights groups or others not specialized in construction. Moreover, minority contractor associations are organized in
almost every major population center in the nation. As of September
1973, associations of minority contractors existed in 118 cities
across the United States. [7]

Utilizing minority contractor associations to furnish listings
of minority contractors makes sense, but it is not without problems.
Individual associations vary considerably as to organization and
capacity. Some associations have to date given little priority to
compiling a complete or accurate list of contractors in their area.
Further, some associations might be reluctant to identify nonmem-
ber contractors lest it increase competition for their own membership. Some associations might refuse to participate in publishing
lists, preferring instead to have customers contact the association
for individual referrals. Finally, it would be unwieldy for the government to contract with each local association individually, and the
national association has not been strong enough to undertake such
an effort alone (although it has the benefit of a good start in the
circulation list for Minority Builder magazine).

Perhaps the best approach would be a well-monitored contract to the NAMC with subcontracts in turn to individual local
associations. This arrangement would have the added benefit of
strengthening the NAMC and furthering its relationship with local
associations. If contracting with NAMC proves unfeasible, an alternative would be to have government agencies compile lists on the
local level on the model of the SFRA effort. Someone of influence who
works closely with procurement and has daily contact with minority
contractors should be made responsible for maintaining and updating
the list and seeing that it is utilized. If contractors need to be
cleared in advance to bid on the agency's projects, technical-assistance efforts need to be added to assure that all available and willing
minority contractors are cleared. Compiling lists should be recognized as only a first step; the key task is to utilize such lists. And
minority contractor associations are in an excellent position to
ensure that listings are utilized. (See Chapter 6 for a fuller discussion of these associations.)

Procurement Conferences

Beyond identifying minority firms, government attempts to
stimulate contracts for minority firms have taken the form of work-

shops to instruct minority contractors in bidding procedures on government projects. Such workshops have been sponsored or co-sponsored by several organizations, including the SBA, the Office of Minority Business Enterprises (OMBE), HUD, and state and local agencies. The programs have usually featured talks by purchasing agents from various government agencies. Some workshops have specifically focused on construction. Others have been designed for any minority business interested in supplying goods or services to the government. Such conferences have been conducted numerous times in each of the cities studied.

For several reasons, procurement workshops have enjoyed limited success in attracting minority contractors to bid and perform government work. First, government agencies that have had low minority participation on past contracts face credibility problems in convincing minorities that bidding procedures are now open to them. Second, since procurement and bidding procedures are generally complex and vary from agency to agency, minority contractors are understandably reluctant to invest in learning when they have little assurance of obtaining contracts for their efforts. Third, inability to obtain bonding has prevented some conference attendants from bidding for government work.

Although procurement conferences have resulted in much frustration for the contractors as well as agency procurement officials, they have played some useful roles, such as providing initial channels of communication between contractors and agencies and serving as forums for minority grievances. Further, procurement conferences provide introductions that can be followed up in more productive one-to-one tutorial relationships. Procurement conferences have also shown that mere information exchange and an open-door policy are insufficient to assure significant participation of minority firms in government work. Thus, other efforts, such as the set-aside, have been pursued.

The Set-Aside

There were precedents for setting aside government contracts for particular groups of firms before the technique was applied to minorities. The U.S. Department of Defense has used set-asides to help support small firms. In addition, under section 8(a) of the Small Business Act of 1953, as amended, the SBA was empowered "to enter into contracts with the United States Government and any Department, Agency, or Offices thereof having procurement powers obligating the Administration to furnish articles, equipment, supplies, or materials to the Government" and "to arrange for the performance of such contracts by negotiating or otherwise letting sub-

contracts to small business concerns or others." In other words,
the SBA may serve as prime contractor to government purchasing
agencies and then subcontract to qualified small firms.

Prodded by the lobbying efforts of minority contractors, the
SBA's 8(a) purchasing program was extended to disadvantaged construction contractors in 1969.

Theoretically, the 8(a) program operates to accomplish its
stated purpose in three ways. First, it affords the recipient contractor an opportunity to prove his ability to undertake large projects that would be unavailable to him through normal channels.
Second, in allowing a contractor to operate near his full capacity,
the 8(a) program permits him to function more efficiently by
spreading his fixed costs over a larger output. Finally, technical
assistance is to be provided to 8(a) contractors, thus enhancing the
training aspects of the 8(a) program.

Despite the laudable objectives of the 8(a) program, interviews in Houston and Atlanta painted a rather unfavorable picture
of the program in 1971. In brief, the program results in Houston
and Atlanta had been meager, largely because of faulty outreach,
resulting partially from inadequate staffing of the program on the
local level, and partially from ineffective efforts on the part of the
existing staff.[8] Among the contractors interviewed, only 28 out of
101 (or 28 percent) were even familiar with the program. Of these
28, 9 had submitted résumés and had been accepted in the program,
and only 2 (both in Houston) had performed work under the program.
Not a single 8(a) contract was found let to a minority contractor in
Atlanta (see Table A.37.)

By 1973-74, when interviews were conducted in Chicago and
San Francisco-Oakland, outreach for the 8(a) program had considerably improved. In these two cities, 136 of 190 (or 72 percent) of
the contractors interviewed were familiar with the program and 61
firms (or 32 percent) had been accepted into the program. The key
problem, however, was lack of 8(a) contracts. Over half of those
accepted for the program had not performed any work under it (see
Table A.37).

Upon further investigation, the author found that the experience of the contractors interviewed was indeed representative of
that of other firms under the program. SBA sources revealed that
as of midsummer 1973, 81 of 135 construction firms with résumés
accepted for the program in federal region IX had not received a
single contract. And some of these firms had been listed for two
years or more. One official argued that it is unrealistic to expect
such a small staff to perform effectively all the functions included
in the SBA role in the program: contract development, outreach,

contractor prequalification, contract negotiation, and follow-up monitoring and technical assistance. [9]

Although lack of available contracts was one of the chief criticisms minority contractors had to offer regarding the program, it was not the only one. Several contractors complained that they were prohibited by local SBA officials from soliciting their own work under the program, although a Washington SBA spokesperson announced that such solicitations were appropriate. [10] Some contractors alleged that costs on 8(a) contract prices were negotiated at unrealistically low levels, and that minority contractors undertaking such work were incurring huge losses. Some interviewees related experiences they had heard from other contractors. Allegedly, some low-priced 8(a) contracts, having been refused by minority contractors, were later put out for regular bid, only to be contracted at prices substantially above the offered 8(a) price. Unfortunately, there were never sufficient details related to enable the author to verify the accusations. However, it is clear that any program such as 8(a) is dependent on good-faith efforts by all parties involved, including the contracting agency for whom the work is to be done.

A major problem with the operations of the 8(a) program was that interagency cooperation essential to success of the program had not been forthcoming. Some agencies, such as HUD, avoided using the program, preferring to operate their own assistance efforts for contractors.* Other agencies, concerned more with getting their contracts completed than with assisting minority firms, participated in the 8(a) program only reluctantly.

Some contractors were pleased with the performance of the 8(a) program but suggested that the SBA increase its staff on the program and obtain persons knowledgeable about construction estimating to assist with agency negotiations on 8(a) contract prices.

As the experience of many minority contractors interviewed bears out, larger government projects offer a good way for minorities to develop a track record on larger projects. Among those who have obtained government work, 40 percent indicated that the largest contracts they had ever performed were public jobs (see Table A.25). Several of these jobs were performed under the 8(a) program.

---

*Under one such effort in Los Angeles, HUD set aside 1,000 units of federally financed housing with a mortgage value of $21 million for minority builders and developers. However, this effort has not been replicated since.

Proponents of demand stimulation as the solution to problems of minority contractors are often surprised to learn that a few of the larger minority contractors reported getting all the business they could handle and were extremely selective about the projects they undertook. It is clear that for a few of the larger minority firms, obtaining jobs was not a problem. In fact, some of the best minority firms were (in a good market) in the enviable position of being able to pick and choose for whom they work—just as do many of the better nonminority firms. And some capable minority contractors are simply not interested in performing government work, especially during good economic times.

The demand-stimulation approach also has inherent limitations. For example, it is often of little help to the promising contractor attempting to break into new work (such as government work, commercial or industrial work, or large contract work) on which he has little or no track record. The supply-development approach is intended for this type of firm.

THE SUPPLY-DEVELOPMENT APPROACH

The supply-development approach to minority contractor upgrading assumes that work is readily available for minority firms if they can qualify to perform it. This approach stresses improving the bonding, financial, and performance capacity of minority firms in construction.

Supply development has taken a variety of forms. Chief among these have been the provision of bonding and financial assistance, managerial and technical assistance, and labor training.

Financial and Bonding Assistance

One of the earliest efforts to deal with the bonding and financial problems of minority contractors was made by the Ford Foundation. Responding to requests for assistance from minority contractors in various parts of the country and to the suggestion of HUD representatives, the Ford Foundation initiated discussions in 1966 with several major surety companies to deal with the bonding problems of minority contractors. As an outcome of these discussions, in June 1968, the General and Specialty Contractors Association (GSCA) of Oakland, California, was financed to establish a revolving loan fund and a bonding-aid program for contractors.[11] The Ford Foundation then attempted to model the program[12] and replicate it in Cleveland, Boston, and New York.[13] The New York City project was the beginning of the Urban Coalition's involvement in programs that later blossomed into the Minority Contractors Assistance Program (MCAP).

Initially formed by the Urban Coalition with the help of the NAMC, MCAP is a Washington-based organization aiming to remedy the financial and bonding programs of minority contractors. In July 1970, MCAP negotiated a $2 million, 15-year loan with five major insurance companies. The loan was supplemented with a $500,000 grant from the Ford Foundation, together with a $390,000 grant from the Economic Development Administration. These resources were made available to local contractor associations to establish revolving loan funds for liquidity capital and technical assistance to member contractors along the lines of the pilot experimental models in Boston, Cleveland, New York City, and Oakland.

In addition to its efforts in providing loan funds to minority contractor associations, MCAP provided technical and managerial assistance to associations as well as some individual minority contractors on larger contracts. [14] It also published guidebooks for use by contractors and their associations, [15] worked with private corporations and government agencies with major building programs to promote participation of minority contractors, [16] and conducted various seminars and workshops on minority construction problems and solutions. [17]

Civil rights groups, such as the National Urban League, the NAACP, and Recruitment and Training Program (RTP) have helped individual minority contractors negotiate, finance, and obtain bonding for projects of significant size. Similar efforts have been made by the Opportunity Funding Corporation (OFC), established in June 1970 with a $7.4 million grant from the Office of Economic Opportunity. As one of its five major activities, the OFC operated a Contractor Bonding Program, which utilized various financial devices—including letters of credit, capital loan guarantees, equity guarantees, and credit-line guarantees—to help minority contractors obtain bonding. None of the contractors interviewed acknowledged receiving any help from these organizations, however.

A few minority contractors have reduced or eliminated their financial problems with the aid of special efforts by local financial institutions to assist minority business. As of the end of 1971, four minority contractors in Atlanta had received financial help from the Community Development Corporation (CDC), a subsidiary of the Citizens and Southern Bank established to make soft loans to disadvantaged businessmen. Sam Pierce, assistant director for CDC in Atlanta, reported that one of the four had grown substantially since being financed. In Chicago, assistance from Hyde Park Bank and Southside Bank, two white-owned institutions that have consciously attempted to increase minority loans, was acknowledged by a few of the contractors interviewed. One of the most publicized private efforts was made in New York. In September 1972, Morgan Guaranty Trust Company set into operation a special Minority Contractors' Program to boost selected minority contractors in New York City from a contract level of $50,000 to a level of $1.5 million over a three-year period.[18] The project sought to build a model program of financial assistance for minority contractors that could be adopted by Morgan's correspondent banks and replicated in other cities. By October 1973, the program had made five loans to minority contractors supporting $3.5 million in contracts.[19] While such efforts are useful and beneficial to a handful of minority contractors, they represent only a drop in the bucket. To make a meaningful contribution toward alleviating the financial problems of minority contractors, far greater efforts on the part of private financial institutions must be forthcoming.

The SBA is the forefront of federal efforts to increase the financial and bonding capacity of minority contractors. Through its economic opportunity and other loan programs, the SBA has attempted to service the financial needs of disadvantaged business-people since the mid-1960s.

Minority contractors in Houston and Atlanta in 1971 were highly critical of SBA performance, however. At that time only 7 of 90 contractors (or 8 percent) had ever received an SBA loan at any time, and none rated SBA as a chief source of financing. Further, contractors expressed considerable criticism regarding available SBA loan programs, emphasizing the following themes:

The loan application process takes too long. The typical waiting period for a successful loan was six months. Only two contractors received a loan within four months. One of these had received a loan in ten days, which helped him start his business; the other stated that he received a $12,500 loan within three weeks. Many of the 15 contractors who failed to obtain a loan simply gave up during the long wait. Many others have never applied for an SBA loan because they had heard fellow contractors complain about the delay.

The loan money is available for what the contractors do not need (to finance establishment of an office or purchase of more equipment) but seemingly never available for what they do need (interim financing to pay for supplies and payroll).

Loans are not large enough to be of any assistance.

Too much paper work is involved in obtaining a loan.[20]

Loans are not available for those who need them. "You can only get a loan if you already have money" was a familiar refrain heard during the interviews.

In 1971, the SBA started two new programs, which were designed recognizing some of the special problems facing disadvantaged contractors in construction. These were the Revokable Revolving Line of Credit Program and the Surety Bond Guarantee Program. Through the former, a qualified contractor could establish with his private bank a line of credit up to $350,000 under an SBA guarantee. Under the Surety Bond Guarantee Program, surety bonds or contracts to $500,000 may be 90 percent guaranteed by the SBA. [21]

Interviews conducted for the study in 1973-74 in Chicago and San Francisco-Oakland offered the opportunity to view the impact of the two new programs and assess any change in contractors' attitudes toward the SBA.

In brief, criticism of SBA loan programs by minority contractors did not abate between 1971 and 1973-74. In fact, for every contractor who had a favorable word to say about the SBA, there was another who offered a mixed opinion, and seven others who had unfavorable comment only.

Although many of the criticisms were much the same as those expressed by southern contractors in 1971, contractors noted some improvements brought about by the new revokable, revolving line-of-credit program. The application process still involved a long delay and much paper work, they insisted, but once approval was granted, the contractors on the program expressed satisfaction with the program because it was specifically designed to provide the sort of funding they need— interim financing. Others stated that "the program is good as far as it goes" but complained that "the money is available for only one job at a time." Such a limitation might be suitable for a general contractor or a large subcontractor, but not for the smaller specialty contractor who performs several jobs at once.

The survey in Chicago and Oakland-San Francisco also indicated that a large portion of minority contractors was unfamiliar with the program as late as 1974. Although most contractors knew generally that the SBA made loans to businesses, more than half had not heard of the line-of-credit program. Sources of information for the ones familiar with the program, in order of frequency, were minority contractor associations, the SBA itself, a bank, or a fellow contractor.

About one out of ten minority contractors interviewed was participating in the program, 4 percent of the contractors considered the SBA to be their chief source of financing.

Knowledge of the Surety Bond Guarantee Program was more widespread, and more contractors interviewed had participated in it. Of 188 respondents, 109 or 58 percent were familiar with the program and 35 had participated in it. (See Table A.37.) One reason for the better outreach on this program is that the 90 percent guarantee has lured several smaller surety companies to serve this guaranteed market. Nationally, as of April 20, 1974, 21,470 guarantees had been granted, resulting in 14,226 contracts obtained. An estimated 40 percent of the guarantees were made to minority contractors. [22]

Aggregate figures regarding participation in the new SBA programs mask important differences by area and minority group. Data collected in contractor interviews as well as SBA data confirm that both programs were more vigorously pursued on the West Coast than in other regions. Efforts needed to be pursued within SBA to increase knowledge of the program in other areas. Moreover, blacks were more familiar with the programs than other minorities, possibly because blacks are better-organized. Efforts were needed with other minorities as well.

Technical and Managerial Assistance

If minority firms in construction are to be upgraded, the provision of technical and managerial assistance to minority contractors is critical. Unfortunately, this appears to be one of the toughest tasks to accomplish.

Attempts to provide technical and managerial assistance to minority contractors have taken a variety of forms. The OMBE has funded business-development groups that have helped contractors individually with such matters as accounting or loan packaging. One of the business-development organizations receiving favorable reviews from contractors is ASIAN, Inc., which served Chinese, Japanese, and Filipino contractors in the Bay area.

In addition to business-development organizations, OMBE developed the specially focused Construction Contractor Assistance Center (CCAC) program, which "provides management and technical assistance and monitors the operations of minority contractors to enable them to acquire bonding, financing, and other resources needed to compete effectively."[23] As of July 1973, OMBE had funded 17 organizations to operate as CCACs. Of these, 13 were lodged with local associations of minority contractors.[24]

Several seminars and classroom workshop series have been held. The Turner Construction Company and others have sponsored classroom courses held in local colleges. Overall, the accomplishments of the classroom efforts have been limited; in fact, some Turner officials indicated reluctance to repeat the experience. One major problem is getting minority contractors to attend such sessions. This, in turn, involves making the sessions meaningful to contractors and finding a convenient time for them.

Technical assistance has taken various other forms. In Los Angeles, a major corporation (outside the construction industry) loaned one of its black executives to assist a group of black contractors. In various cities across the country, the SBA enlists the help of active businesspeople and retired executives through its ACE and SCORE programs. The U.S. Department of Labor had funded the Latin American Construction Contractors of Chicago, who have in turn sponsored a preparation course for licensing exams in plumbing. United Builders of Chicago established a Model Cities-funded technical-assistance effort. Primarily this has in practice meant assistance with estimating and bidding.

Data from interviews showed technical assistance to be critical because many minority contractors get into business with little more than an excellent knowledge of their craft. Few had supervisory experience with larger construction projects, prior business training, or polished business skills. A major exception has been a small core of established southern black contractors who graduated from vocational programs in black colleges which taught them how to establish their own firms in a world that would not hire them as employees. However, as job opportunities for black college graduates have improved, black colleges have revised their curricula to take the focus off preparing graduates for self-employment.

Person-to-person on-the-job tutorial efforts between individuals who have established relationships over time seem to work well. Contractors interviewed expressed preference for on-the-job training dealing with concrete problems specific to their firms rather than general classroom instruction. The diversity of minority firms, each with particular problems, requires a wide array of technical assistance and individualized attention. Uncovered in this study were many examples of individual efforts of white contractors or employees of major firms to provide technical assistance. One white electrical contractor in Atlanta taught a fellow black contractor how to bid and estimate by checking over his bid. In Chicago, a key employee with estimating and management skills of a major firm has effectively provided technical assistance on a one-to-one basis to a few promising black subcontractors. An established white contractor in Berkeley has joined at least two struggling black firms as a long-term "low profile" partner. Meaningful joint ventures between white firms and minority firms in Chicago and the San Francisco Bay area have similarly provided learning opportunities for several minority contractors. At a minimum, effective tutorial efforts require an atmosphere of mutual respect and trust. Only in such an environment is communication and learning possible.

A source for increasing numbers of minority contractors is the pool of apprenticeship graduates placed through apprenticeship outreach organizations. The RTP of New York City, one of the oldest existing outreach organizations, reports that already some of the apprenticeship graduates it has placed have moved up to become contractors on their own.[25] Similarly, the staff of United Builders of Chicago has worked with apprenticeship graduates originally placed by the Urban League LEAP program in that city to develop some of the most promising young minority firms in that city, including the only black-owned structural-steel contractor identified in fieldwork for this study.

Other potential sources of training for future minority contractors are the courses and programs currently offered in construction management and construction technology in 83 colleges and universities across the nation.[26] Greater affirmative-action efforts are needed to ensure meaningful minority enrollment in these programs.

Labor Training

Coordinating manpower training for the disadvantaged with a minority business-development program has great appeal. At least one recent study has alluded to the potential benefits of doing just this.[27] In construction, this idea has the added appeal of offering a method of integrating building-trades unions.

Some experience with combining job training with business development has been accumulated. The original labor training effort among minority contractors was Project UPGRADE in Oakland. Since UPGRADE, labor training programs operated by minority contractors have been funded through the JOBS program (either on an individual firm or consortium basis), Model Cities programs, and direct grants from the Department of Labor, such as the Latin American Task Force in Chicago in 1973. In addition, since minority contractor associations fit the definition of community-based organizations under the Comprehensive Employment and Training Act of 1973 (CETA), they have become candidates for funding from state and local CETA prime sponsors.

For a variety of reasons, the results of these labor training efforts have been mixed; in practice, the programs fall far short of their goals and conceptual ideals. Some programs have been badly implemented. Unions have generally resisted specialized training programs in construction, viewing them as second-rate training designed to circumvent the apprenticeship system. NAB-JOBS officials in Chicago and San Francisco relate that for both areas together only eight JOBS programs had been performed in construction through 1974 and that all future programs in construction required written concurrences from union business agents. Graduates of Project UPGRADE in Oakland had trouble joining the union upon graduation. Even though the project was cosponsored by the Alameda Building and Construction Trades Council, individual local unions refused to cooperate with it. Officials of State Apprenticeship Councils (SAC) and the U.S. Bureau of Apprenticeship and Training (BAT) have denied trainee certification to Project UPGRADE and other programs operated by minority contractors. Lacking such certification, trainees are refused GI Bill benefits, and contractors must pay full journeyman scale to all trainees of government jobs covered by the Davis-Bacon Act. BAT and SAC officials charge that such programs have inadequate related training components, exploit workers, and do not prepare graduates to undertake work as full-status journeymen. UPGRADE officials deny the charges. Unfortunately, lacking hard data on the experience of past graduates of the UPGRADE program, it is difficult to weigh the arguments on each side of the controversy. Even if perfect information were available, the emotional nature of the controversy had hardened positions so that a solution without third-party intervention was unlikely to be achieved even by negotiation. In January 1976, with the Oakland construction market on the skids and several journeymen out of work, training additional minority craftworkers through Project UPGRADE became untenable. Thus it temporarily suspended operations. By April 1977, the suspension was still in effect.

One conclusion stands out from this review of labor training efforts by minority contractors. Union resistance to minority contractor training efforts has driven many minority contractors to join ranks with nonunion contractors and nonunion organizations such as ABC and the Associated Independent Electrical Contractors (AIEC) to solve their training problems. By 1977, overtures in this direction had been made by minority contractors in every city studied. Where such efforts will lead, of course, depends on future relationships between unions and minority contractors.

Interviews with contractors provided a good picture of training efforts which have been undertaken by individual minority firms.

In Houston and Atlanta, few minority contractors have formal training programs for their employees. In Atlanta, 9 firms out of 38 interviewed have some sort of training program for their employees. Of these nine, four participated in union apprenticeship programs, two had contracts with the JOBS program (one in masonry and one in tile), one had a trainee from the government industrial-education center, and one had a veterans' on-the-job training (OJT) program. One of the contractors conducted formal classes in blueprint reading for his employees in his own home. These findings revealed a higher incidence of training than those uncovered by the NAACP survey, which found four of twenty-two contractors involved in formal training programs, two of which were union apprenticeship.

In Houston, participation in formal training programs was much lower among Mexican-Americans. Out of forty-five Mexican-American contractors, only three had participated in any formal training efforts. Two of these had participated in union apprenticeship with Plumbers Local 68 (one of whom had withdrawn from the program before the interview). The third was applying to train a draftsman under a Model Cities vocational-guidance program. Black contractors in Houston had more experience with formal training programs. Out of 11 contractors interviewed, 4 had participated in formal training programs (none was union apprenticeship). One program was for ten air-conditioning helpers; another was a Crescent Foundation (a nonprofit black training organization) manpower program; the fourth was a private drafting course provided by a local vocational-education school teacher who was also the president of the Houston Association of General and Sub-Contractors. The NAACP survey of black contractors found that 9 of 78 contractors in Houston had participated in some type of formal training program.

In contrast to Houston and Atlanta, where only 16 of 94 contractors (or 17 percent) engaged in formal training programs for their employees, 72 of the 186 non-South contractors (or 39 percent) reported that they provided some sort of formal training to their employees. In Chicago, more than half of the employers who train participated in apprenticeship. One black contractor had participated in training efforts of the Illinois state vocational-education program. Five other black contractors provided semistructured training of one sort or another to their employees. The most interesting was that provided by an older union plumber who performed small residential jobs. He took on young men in a tutorial situation, trained them, and then subcontracted jobs to them. He claimed to have spawned several contractors in this manner. Among Spanish-American contractors, one of the associations, Progressive Builders, ran classes for a while, providing general orientation to youngsters interested in construction; but this effort was abandoned reportedly because the teacher found it too burdensome to travel in from the suburbs for every class. The other association of Spanish-American contractors, Latin American Contractors Consortium, also ran classes for workers studying for the plumbing license exam; but none of the contractors interviewed mentioned this program.

In the San Francisco area, training took the form of participation in Project UPGRADE or PREP or in various governmental programs run through a Model Cities program or the SFRA. The latter type of program received mixed reviews. Smaller contractors appeared to be generally pleased with them, whereas larger contractors complained that the salary incentive offered in these programs was too low and that the selection process for trainees was poor.

Very few contractors in the San Francisco area reported participating in apprenticeship programs. Yet, in response to the question, "Where do your workers get their training?," most answered "union apprenticeship." This held true even among contractors who had participated in government training programs. Few acknowledged government training as a primary source of training for their workers.

As to the form of the training most desirable, the minority contractors were in general agreement that an apprenticeship-style program of training—combining classroom work with on-the-job learning—was the best format for skill-acquisition in the construction industry. Many contractors in the non-South who were apprenticeship graduates made favorable comments regarding their own training.

Contractors expressed a wide variety of attitudes about participating in worker training programs themselves. One interviewee in the San Francisco area was so enthusiastic about his trade that he had volunteered to teach a course in it at a local community college. On the other hand, a Chicago contractor, discussing his experience with a training project for disadvantaged youth in Lawndale, commented: "I learned there that you can't mix sociology and business." When another contractor was asked if he would be interested in participating in some labor training program, he stated, "I would if I could see that I could make money on it."

On the one hand, it would appear to be unwise to load a marginal contractor, struggling to maintain existence, with the burden of training a disadvantaged work force. On the other hand, many of the minority contractors are under significant pressures from their own communities to hire and train fellow minorities; and they are training anyway, whether or not they receive government assistance.

Noting that employment in minority construction enterprise is highly concentrated among a few firms, it would seem that the numbers of minority contractors able to sponsor training adequately are limited in number. Or to put it another way, by locating training efforts selectively among the few larger minority contractors, the government would be reaching the vast majority of workers employed by all minority construction enterprise.

As noted in Chapter 2, the employment-generating potential of minority contractors varies significantly by place and trade. Hence the potential of minority firms to influence the ethnic and racial composition of union memberships varies substantially by trade and geographic area as well.

In some areas, minority contractors may have significant impact in increasing minority participation among building-trades unions. As testified to in interviews with contractors and union officials, contractors do have some leverage in the matter of getting employees into the union; and some minority contractors have used this leverage. The extent of leverage a contractor has, of course, is determined by several considerations, such as the size of his firm, his own personal background with the union, personality, and current labor market conditions.

Although minority employment in minority-owned firms is substantially above minority employment levels in Anglo-owned firms (see Table A.28), relying on minority contractors to integrate the building trades may be unwarranted for several reasons: in trades in which the unions have the fewest minority members, minority contractors are generally scarce too; although three-quarters of the existing minority contractors want to expand their businesses, only a fourth of these firms aspires to work in unionized (primarily large commercial and industrial construction) sectors; and the larger a minority construction firm grows, the smaller the proportion of minority workers it tends to employ. In fact, affirmative-action officers and contractors in San Francisco and Chicago pointed out several minority-owned firms with lower percentages of minority workers than nonminority firms bidding against them.[28]

In summary, although minority firms may assist in increasing minority participation in the building trades, in most places, their effort would not be significant enough in itself to integrate the trades. Efforts still need to be made through other approaches,

such as apprenticeship outreach programs to recruit and place
minority youngsters into union apprenticeships and legal and administrative equal employment opportunity pressures to promote affirmative action.

CONCLUSIONS

Demand-stimulation efforts in the form of publishing directories of minority firms and redirecting government and private procurement, and supply-development efforts including bonding and
financial assistance, technical and managerial assistance, and
labor training, have all been directed at upgrading minority enterprise in construction. Each has encountered difficulties on the
practical level.

Even in theory, however, relying exclusively on either
demand stimulation or supply development alone will not move
minority contractors into the mainstream of the construction industry. What are needed are efforts to cope with both demand and
supply problems. Two promising vehicles for accomplishing this—
the joint venture and the minority contractors' association—are the
subject of discussion in the next two chapters.

NOTES

1.   Joseph Debro, "The Minority Builder," Labor Law
Journal 21 (May 1970): 301.

2.   Daniel Quinn Mills, Industrial Relations and Manpower
in Construction (Cambridge, Mass.: MIT Press, 1970), pp. 174-75.

3.   Reginald Stuart, "Construction Lag Hurts Minority
Builders," New York Times, June 17, 1974.

4.   Memorandum from Jerry T. Dawson, deputy affirmative
action officer, UDC, to Dr. Kenneth Clark, chairman, Affirmative
Action Committee, entitled "Affirmative Action Summary Report,"
dated July 8, 1974, p. 2.

5.   A statistical summary of the work with Spanish-American professionals was published by Juarez and Associates. See A
Report: National Survey of Minority Professionals and Businesses
in Housing Production and Urban Development (Los Angeles: Juarez
and Associates, 1972).

6.   See Guide to Minority Business Directories, annual editions (available from National Minority Business Campaign, 1016
Plymouth Avenue, Minneapolis, Minn. 55411).

7.   A listing of such associations, the most complete available to September 1973, was compiled for this study. Probably the best regularly published listing of associations may be found in Try Us, annual editions (available from the National Minority Business Campaign, 1016 Plymouth Avenue, North, Minneapolis, Minn. 55411).

8.   Further detail on the operation of the 8(a) program in Houston and Atlanta in 1971 is contained in Robert W. Glover, "Developing and Upgrading Minority Construction Contractors: The Atlanta and Houston Experiences," Ph.D. dissertation, University of Texas, 1972.

9.   Confidential communication, 1973.

10.   Statement of Joseph Conrad, director, Minority Contractors Development Program, Small Business Administration, to the National Association of Minority Contractors Regional Conference in Houston, January 5, 1973.

11.   "Grant Promotes Minority Builders," Engineering News-Record, July 11, 1968.

12.   See Douglas Pugh and Matthew Domber, Minority Contractors Bonding Program: A Manual of Organizational Steps and Procedures (New York: Ford Foundation, Division of National Affairs, 1968), p. 2.

13.   Douglas C. Pugh, "Bonding Minority Contractors," in Black Economic Development, ed. William F. Haddad and Douglas Pugh (Englewood Cliffs, N.J.: Prentice-Hall, 1969) pp. 138-50.

14.   Personal interview with Thomas Brown, director of technical assistance, MCAP, Washington, D.C., July 31, 1973.

15.   See, for example, Minority Contractors Assistance Project, Standard Record-Keeping Procedures for Contractors (Washington, D.C.: Minority Contractors Assistance Project and the National Urban Coalition, updated) and MCAP Guidelines for Increasing Minority Participation in the Construction Industry (Washington, D.C.: Minority Contractors Assistance Project, undated.).

16.   As one example of this type of activity, MCAP is assisting implementation of an interagency agreement (among HUD, OMBE, and the SBA) "to help furnish information, training, and financial aid to small and minority group home repair contractors who want to get involved in HUD's property disposition program." MCAP's particular role will be to provide followup training for minority contractors. See "HUD, OMBE, and SBA Project to Employ Minority Contractors in Home Repair," Fair Employment Report, July 1, 1974, p. 12.

17.   For further details regarding the MCAP effort, see "Black Hardhats Organize: The Story of Minority Contractors Assistance Project," Black Business Digest, March 1972, pp. 22-24, 59.

18.   Morgan Guaranty Trust Company, "Morgan's Guaranty's Minority Contractors' Program" (New York: Morgan Guaranty Trust Company, undated), mimeographed, p. 1.

19.   Personal correspondence from Woodie G. Williams, assistant vice-president, Morgan Guaranty Trust Company, New York, dated October 17, 1973.

20.   At least one study has found that the paper work and unfamiliar forms used by the SBA have even deterred bankers from participating in SBA loan programs. See Albert Shapero, Cary Hoffman, Kirk P. Draheim, and Richard P. Howell, The Role of the Financial Community in the Formation, Growth, and Effectiveness of Technical Companies (Austin: Multi-Disciplinary Research, Inc., for the Ozarks Regional Commission, 1969), p. 50.

21.   Information on the SBA Bonding Guarantee Program is detailed in the article, "The SBA Bond Guarantee," Black Enterprise, February 1972, p. 54.

22.   Telephone interview with Sal A. Lauricella, director, Surety Bond Guarantee Program, Washington, D.C., May 13, 1974.

23.   Office of Minority Business Enterprise, OMBE Funded Organizations (Washington, D.C.: Government Printing Office, 1973), p. 5.

24.   Personal interview with William Brewster, OMBE, Washington, D.C., July 31, 1973.

25.   Cited in "Training Minority Craftsmen," Minority Builder, May/June, 1974, p. 6.

26.   A listing of schools of higher education offering construction curricula is provided in Construction Education Directory, 2d. ed. (Washington, D.C.: The Associated General Contractors of America, Education and Research Foundation, 1974).

27.   Vernon John Dixon, "A Determination of Investment Priorities in Urban Black Communities: Bedford-Stuyvesant," Ph.D. dissertation, Princeton University, 1973.

28.   Personal interviews with Chet V. Brookins, labor relations and EEO officer, Henry C. Beck Company, San Francisco, January 28, 1974, and with Stanley Lim, employment representative, Human Rights Commission of San Francisco, San Francisco, May 16, 1972.

CHAPTER 5

JOINT VENTURES

Joint venturing is a common business practice in the construction industry. Of the white contractors interviewed for this study, 40 percent had participated in at least one joint venture—all with other white-owned firms (see Table A.39). Most joint ventures are undertaken either to enable several companies to perform a project beyond their individual capacity, but many other reasons may prompt a firm to enter into a joint-venture agreement. Even Brown and Root, Inc., one of the largest construction firms in the world, has joint-ventured with small rural contractors located near a construction site in order to acquire a contract for obtaining nonunion local labor.[1]

In general, contractors enter into joint-venture agreements in order to achieve a mutual sharing of talents, capabilities, or contracts. Thus, white contractors are motivated to joint-venture with minority firms to gain access to the minority community in order to meet their affirmative-action requirements on a job. For example, Turner Construction Company joint-ventured with Trans-Bay Builders and Engineers—a predominantly black firm—on their Oakland Redevelopment Projects to gain access to the East Bay minority construction community.

Overall, joint venturing appears to have considerable appeal to minority contractors. More than three out of four contractors interviewed indicated their willingness to joint-venture in one form or another at some point in the future (see Table A.40).

Black contractors in Chicago, who, as a group, had the most frequent experience with joint venturing, expressed the greatest willingness to joint-venture in the future; more than nine out of ten were in favor of doing so.

96

The contractors interviewed expressed a variety of reasons for joint venturing: to pool work, to obtain contracts beyond their firm's financial or working capacity, to gain knowledge and experience, to gain something essential to winning or performing a contract, and to perform projects with a contractor in a complementary trade. (For example, a plumber sought to joint-venture with an air-conditioning contractor in order to submit a bid for all mechanical contracting work in a particular project, and a carpentery contractor was interested in joint-venturing with a plumber and an electrical contractor in order to specialize in remodeling doctors' offices.)

Joint ventures, strictly speaking, are temporary alliances arranged for the duration of one construction project only or for some specified time period. Under a joint venture, each firm retains its individual identity but operates with the other(s) as a unit to accomplish the job. Joint ventures involving more than two firms are sometimes called "consortiums."

Many forms of joint venture exist. For example, there are minority-nonminority or minority-minority joint ventures. Moreover, there is a continuum in the form of possible types of combinations, ranging from temporary schemes for one project only to full-scale limited mergers.

MINORITY-NONMINORITY JOINT VENTURES

One promising route for upgrading minority contractors is joint venturing with larger white contractors. Such ventures may provide a means to develop a track record by providing minority firms with experience on larger commercial or industrial projects. Further, Debro contends, "As a method of financing a minority contractor, the joint venture technique is without parallel. It takes full advantage of the resources available from the nonminority community, while at the same time it does not require a dilution of minority contractor equity or control."[2]

Joint venturing with white contractors is popularly cited as a way of upgrading minority firms.[3] Moreover, white contractors and their spokespersons outside the South who have experience with joint venturing with minorities advocate it as possibly the only way that minority firms will be upgraded.[4]

White contractors are motivated to look for minority firms to fulfill affirmative-action requirements. But some are concerned more with image than with providing real assistance to the minority. Likewise, some minority contractors are content to go along with the game, place their signs and/or trailers on the project site, and drop by on paydays to collect their easy pay.

The financial allure of sham joint venturing is difficult for some marginal minority contractors to resist. One of Chicago's black contractors sympatheized with such behavior: "Why not agree to a quick $10,000 on a sham joint venture when you work hard on other projects and don't make a dime?"

When a minority contractor agrees to participate in such a sham joint venture, he eliminates a possible opportunity for a fellow minority to learn from such an experience. Recognizing this fact, contractors associated with Operation PUSH in Chicago have decided to boycott any sham joint-venture opportunities so that majority contractors would have to offer meaningful participation. At the time of the interview, however, groups were still debating among themselves over the minimum qualifications of a meaningful joint venture—by no means a simple matter. [5]

To avoid sham joint ventures, AAT&TC in Atlanta has discouraged its membership from participating in joint ventures for one project only. Instead, AAT&TC fosters joint ventures of a more permanent nature. In 1975, Herbert Williams, AAT&TC executive director, was able to point to two such long-term arrangements which had worked successfully for more than a year. [6]

Many minority contractors interviewed expressed general reluctance to enter minority-nonminority ventures unless they provide earning as well as learning possibilities. As one black contractor in Atlanta stated:

> I have had many offers from white contractors to joint-venture, but none have favorable terms to me. Some just want me to do the work while they take a slice of the contract. Others are just using me to fulfill their racial quotas for employment. Instead of integrating their own work forces, they want to hire me and my work force.

A cautious approach to joint venturing is not unreasonable. John Brown, president of the black contractors' association in Los Angeles, recalls some of the disappointments his members have experienced in joint venturing with white contractors. [7] He cites the example of a black general contractor who, seeking to establish a track record for bonding on future projects, formed a corporation to joint-venture with a white contractor on a large public housing project. The job went smoothly: upon its completion, the corporation was dissolved as planned. Everything about the venture looked successful until the black contractor applied for bonding on his next project and found that the bonding credit had gone to the joint corporation; when it was dissolved, the track record for bonding also

vanished. Another common pitfall in joint venturing is that the
minority contractor participates only partially in the project.
Brown notes that in several joint ventures, the white contractor
put up the bonding and financing for the project and handled the
bidding and office work while the black contractor effectively became the field superintendent on the job (sometimes even drawing a
regular salary). In such cases, bonding companies consider the
limited participation of the black person as insufficient experience
for future bonding credit. Bonding officials reasoned that although
the black person may have shown great abilities as a field superintendent, he did not necessarily demonstrate his qualification to
tackle an entire contract of equal size as the sole contractor.

However, some joint ventures with white contractors have
been rewarding. A black contractor in San Francisco interviewed
for this study had been able to push his bonding capacity to $300,000
largely as a result of the track record he had established in two
joint ventures on million-dollar projects. Paul King of United
Builders in Chicago relates that one of his firms, Amalgamated
Painting Contractors, gathered many educational benefits in a
joint venture with Hoffman Decorating and Painting Company, a
white firm, on a $200,000 high-rise project in the ghetto. [8]

Among contractors interviewed, joint-venture experience
received varied evaluations. One out of four contractors interviewed
for this study indicated that he had joint-ventured. Exactly half of
these (or one out of eight) had joint-ventured with a white firm.
(See Table A.39.) For every two contractors who spoke positively
about their venture(s), one contractor expressed negative or mixed
feelings about the experience.

Apparently, under the proper conditions joint venturing with
white firms can be advantageous to minority contractors. Joint
venturing with white contractors can be a useful technique for upgrading minority contractors if certain precautions are heeded,
namely: [9]

One party is designated as the managing partner. Early experiences of Spanish-American contractors in the Mission Contractors Association of San Francisco bore out the necessity for having
only one in control. This is especially true in the field. One Chicago
contractor reported that in his experience, it was relatively easy
for upper-level management to get together; but many difficulties
developed among supervisors and crews in the field.

The contractors must mutually participate fully in all phases
of the project. This usually means that the minority puts up bonding
and provides financing and office and field managerial assistance to

its capacity. In doing this, the minority contractor not only gains valuable experiences with all phases of the work but also strengthens his track record for future bonding and financing.

It is best if both contractors can contribute equally to the project, but in cases where there is unequal contribution, the proceeds should be divided proportionately to the contributions.

The arrangement should benefit both contractors. As Paul King of the United Builders of Chicago advises: "Joint venturing should be both a learning and an earning experience for the minority contractor."[10] Benevolent participation on the part of the white contractor in joint venturing does not work either. Concretely, this means that if a white contractor contributes 85 percent to a project, he or she should gain 85 percent of the project returns.

In general, separate corporations should not be established for joint venturing. This caveat is especially important if the minority contractor expects to receive credit for the project for bonding or some other purpose.* In most places, a limited partnership arrangement may be best, since it enables the larger partner to limit his risk while permitting the smaller contractor to gain bonding and financial credit for the experience. Each contractor remains separate and individually intact in this arrangement. However, laws on limited partnership differ from place to place; so in some states, limited partnerships may not be advisable.

Joint ventures should be undertaken only under written contract and with the counsel of a qualified lawyer. A minority contractor should never enter such an arrangement legally blind; his attorney should draw up the contract or at least check it over. (If he does not have an attorney at this stage, he should retain one.) All terms of the agreement should be carefully designed and clearly stated prior to undertaking any work.

Ray Dones, a principal of Trans-Bay Engineers, Inc., a firm with considerable joint-venture experience, has detailed some of the provisions that ought to be included in a joint-venture agreement. The checklist is important enough to bear repeating here:

1. a provision naming the actual contracting organizations (whether or not the construction contract is performed under a separately named entity) to avoid any under-the-table arrangements;
2. arrangements for establishing a separate fund in a special ear-

---

*Of course, if gaining experience is not a factor and if the motivation is only to pool work or some other consideration, it might be fine to incorporate—but in any case, this should only be done with proper legal advice.

marked bank account to finance the venture (the account
should be under dual control and the amounts to be contribu-
ted by each party should be explicit in the initial agreement);

3. a provision requiring all progress payments to be deposited in
this account, including a formal directive to the paying agency to ensure that this provision is carried out;

4. a clause indicating what proportion each party will contribute
in case additional working capital is required;

5. a clause covering contribution and use of equipment on the project, including mention of rental rates, provision for maintenance, and responsibility for downtime;

6. explicit delineation of distribution of profits and losses;

7. provision outlining all duties of the parties, including the managerial duties of the managing partner as well as procedures
to be followed in dealing with unusual situations or problems
that may develop;

8. a clause providing that all parties to the joint venture sign all
necessary documents relating to the contract—bank loans,
bonds, condemnity agreements, and the like;

9. a provision concerning the taking on of additional work or the
purchasing of new equipment during the life of the joint
venture by any of the parties;

10. arrangements for a separate set of books for the joint venture,
to be audited by an outside certified public accountant, preferably one not normally employed by any of the parties;

11. arrangements in case of death or insolvency of any of the
principal parties;

12. a provision covering disposal of equipment and material that
are the property of the joint venture. [11]

Dones argues that joint ventures should be set up with extreme
care because "each co-venture in a joint venture is legally liable for
the performance of the entire contract and the payment of all labor,
material, equipment and other obligations. In other words, if all
but one of the joint ventures fail financially, the remaining joint
venturer is responsible for completing the contract. "[12]

Joint venturing between nonminority and minority parties has
taken place primarily outside the South. The present survey did not
find a single joint venture between a minority contractor and a white
contractor in Houston or Atlanta in 1971, whereas almost one in five
minority contractors in Chicago and in the San Francisco area had
such experience by 1974. Since 1971, there have been a handful of
joint ventures in the southern cities, but not to the extent found in the
North.

However, mere incidence of minority-white joint ventures cannot be taken absolutely as a measure of progress. Some joint ventures are outright sham arrangements, wherein the minority party

gets paid for letting his or her name be used while the white partner maintains complete control over the project. Also, some qualified minority contractors who have won bids have been requested to obtain white joint-venture partners by apprehensive general contractors—not because they objectively need one but merely to calm the general contractor's fears about working with a minority firm. Such experiences have prompted Jesse Jackson of Operation PUSH to label joint ventures "the new jazz."[13]

Nevertheless, some joint ventures with white contractors have been beneficial to minority contractors, and some have carried ancillary benefits. A black painting contractor in San Francisco established a close personal relationship with one of the large white painting contractors in town. As a result, whenever the black contractor got into difficulties over an unjust decision by an inspector or job superintendent, the white contractor came in to vouch for him.[14]

Joint venturing is not the only means of enlisting support of white construction firms in the effort to upgrade minority contractors, but it is a primary way offering much potential.

THIRD-TIER CONTRACTING

One procedure used as an alternative to joint venturing has been the process of awarding third-tier contracts, whereby part of a contractor's work is broken off and contracted to a "sub-subcontractor."

Persons interviewed had some limited experience with this procedure, and some conclusions can be drawn from their comments. Third-tier contracting offers the theoretical advantage of preserving the autonomy of the individual minority firm while offering it limited exposure to larger work. Although success is possible with a third-tier arrangement, the procedure seems to operate well only when the work to be allocated on the third tier is fairly discrete, such as painting stairwells. However, even then the arrangement may have some pitfalls. For example, when one minority contractor in San Francisco lost money on his third-tier contract, allegedly because of unfamiliarity with larger work, he charged the white general and white subcontractor with conspiring to split off the least desirable, least profitable work while they kept the lucrative portions for themselves.

JOINT VENTURES BETWEEN MINORITY FIRMS

A minority contractor may also joint-venture or merge with a fellow minority contractor to their mutual advantage. All of the minority contractors in Houston and Atlanta who had joint-ventured

had done so with other minority firms. Wheatstreet Gardens, a
$2 million housing project—the first built in Atlanta under HUD's
rent-supplement program—was constructed by a team of three
black contractors. One of the three, A. V. Jett, has since pooled
his resources with two other black contractors to form Bankhead
West, Inc., in order to solicit additional large contracts. Reluctant
to give up their own successful individual businesses but anxious
to pursue the possibilities of Bankhead West, the contractors are
entering the corporation as a second business. Each will retain his
own firm with smaller projects until Bankhead West requires his
full attention. In this way, they are able to test the market for
large projects with a minimum of risk to themselves. Shortly after
forming, Bankhead West was able to obtain three Model Cities
housing projects involving an estimated $5,235,000 of work. Al-
though they were experiencing some marketing and bonding difficulties, the firm was still in existence in 1975. [15]

Numerous other, perhaps less dramatic, cases of mergers
or joint ventures between minority contractors were uncovered in
this survey. In all, 41 firms out of 288 (or 14 percent) had undertaken some type of joint venture with a fellow minority contractor.
Most of the participants were pleased with their experience and
willing to repeat it.

Not all joint ventures between minority firms have worked
out well, however. For example, several of the Afro-American
builders' groups established with the assistance and encouragement
of the NAACP have since fallen apart. On August 15, 1973, Robert
Easley reported that groups of Afro-American builders formed to
joint-venture in Buffalo, Hartford, and Birmingham had broken up
or were in the process of breaking up. [16] Rather than proving joint
ventures to be a failure, the demise of the Afro-American builders'
groups may just illustrate the fallacy of undertaking joint ventures
with too many partners. One Chicago contractor experienced in
joint ventures emphasized that two is the optimum number for such
an undertaking. "Any more than that just multiplies the problems
involved," he explained.

NOTES

1.   Personal interview with Joe Huacuja, formerly assistant
manager of the Building Department, Brown and Root Construction
Company, Houston, May 5, 1971.
2.   Joseph Debro, "Financing Minority Contractors,"
Bankers Magazine 154 (Winter 1971): 75.

3.   See Reginald Stuart, <u>Black Contractors' Dilemma</u> (Nashville, Tenn.: Race Relations Information Center, 1971), pp. 21–22; Daniel Quinn Mills, <u>Industrial Relations and Manpower Construction</u> (Cambridge, Mass.: MIT Press, 1972).

4.   Personal interviews with Frank H. Anderson, project manager, Turner Construction Company, Oakland, January 23, 1974; Edward M. Hogan, Jr., assistant secretary, Building Construction Employers Association of Chicago, Chicago, February 28, 1973; Chet V. Brookins, labor relations and EEO officer, Henry C. Beck Co., San Francisco, January 28, 1974; telephone interview with Roy Van Pelz, project manager, F. P. Lathrop Construction, Emeryville, Calif., January 15, 1974.

5.   Personal interview with William M. Smith, Jr., city planner, Andrew Heard and Associates, Ltd. and organizer for Operation PUSH, March 12, 1974.

6.   Telephone interview with Herbert Williams, executive director, Atlanta Associated Contractors and Trades Council, Inc., Atlanta, April 16, 1975.

7.   Personal interview with John Brown, president, Los Angeles Association of General, Sub, and Specialty Contractors, Los Angeles, December 30, 1970.

8.   Personal interview with Paul King, executive director, United Builders Association of Chicago, New Orleans, September 25, 1971.

9.   This discussion was benefited greatly by comments made by John Brown.

        Joint ventures are also common among architectural and engineering firms working in construction. For a practical guide for avoiding pitfalls in ventures between these types of firms, see David R. Dibner, <u>Joint Ventures for Architects and Engineers</u> (New York: McGraw-Hill, 1972).

10.   Personal interview with Paul King.

11.   For a fuller explanation of these provisions, see Ray Dones, "Joint Ventures," <u>Minority Builder</u> 3 (May–June 1973): 21.

12.   Ibid.

13.   Jesse Jackson in a speech before the regional convention of the NAMC, Chicago, June 22, 1973.

14.   Confidential communication, 1974.

15.   Telephone interview with Herbert Williams, executive director, AAT&TC, Atlanta, April 16, 1975.

16.   Telephone interview with Robert Easley, NAACP national office, New York, August 15, 1973.

6

MINORITY CONTRACTOR ASSOCIATIONS

A significant development in the field of minority enterprise during the past decade has been the emergence of local minority contractors' associations across the nation. A survey made in September 1973 by the Center for the Study of Human Resources at the University of Texas identified 118 associations of minority contractors in various stages of formation located in 103 cities across 34 states.[1] All but a handful of these associations had been initiated since 1965.

Trade associations are neither novel nor unusual in the construction industry. Construction probably has more trade associations and fragmentary business groupings than any other industry in the nation.[2] Furthermore, groups such as the AGC and the National Association of Homebuilders have been around a long time and are well known to the public. What is new is that minority firms are beginning to awaken to the benefits of forming trade associations.

The formation of trade associations among contractors—minority or nonminority—stems from a recognition that construction is a unique industry with unusual characteristics and problems, including severe market instability compounded by problems of weather seasonality in production, one-of-a-kind production on ever-changing worksites, strong craft unions, and vulnerability to changes in government policy. Facing such an uncertain environment, businesspeople naturally associate to deal with their problems on an organized basis.

Long excluded from membership in traditional construction trade associations, either by inability to pay the high dues required or occasionally by outright discrimination, minority firms have recently begun to form their own organizations.

In 1964, there were only two minority construction associations—the Associated Electricians of Detroit and the Amalgamated Plumbers Association of Philadelphia—both organized along craft lines. During the next three years, organizations open to contractors of all construction trades were formed in Oakland, Los Angeles, New York, Cleveland, Boston, and a few other cities. Encouraged by the example of these early associations, stimulated by direct organizing efforts of government agencies such as the SBA's Action Construction Team Program, of civil rights groups such as local chapters of the Urban League, or the NAACP, the League of United Latin American Citizens (LULAC), or of the NAMC or other local associations, and lured by the possibility of obtaining funding from governmental or foundation sources, more than 100 organizations of minority contractors were formed from 1967 to 1973. Many of these associations remain in early formative stages and many are fragile organizations operating on shoestring budgets and largely dependent on the efforts of one individual. However, minority contractors' responsiveness to organizations indicates their intentions and hopes to grow and develop their businesses.

Some of the associations sprang from worker-oriented civil rights organizations. Eventually, such organizations generally have split with the original group over worker-management issues or ideological controversies. Thus the Central Contractors Association of Seattle, the Contractors Association of Boston, and the Latin American Construction Contractors of Chicago have all become independent of the worker groups which initially organized them.

Most of the associations have been organized around immediate needs of the contractors. The most common focus of organization has been job procurement; and thus organization of local associations has been strongest and most successful in periods of recession in local construction markets (especially residential work). Although lack of jobs has been the predominant need of contractors, other issues have also played roles in motivating contractors to band together. For example, in Miami, Florida, Cuban contractors organized the Latin Builders Association primarily to pressure the Miami licensing establishment to provide examinations in Spanish. In Lubbock, Texas, a group of Mexican-American contractors organized to establish a cooperative supply company for building materials.

CHARACTERISTICS

Like their nonminority counterparts, minority contractors' associations are trade associations; but they generally place greater emphasis on education of their membership than does the typical trade association. Such emphasis on education stems from the key objectives of minority associations—to develop new minority contractors and help them get into business on a good footing and to assist existing minority firms to grow and perform jobs at a profit.

Minority contractor associations exist in many forms. A few, such as the Afro-American Builders of Virginia or the Conglomerates Construction Company, Inc., in Bridgeport, Connecticut, are for-profit joint ventures of several black contractors who pool their resources to do larger jobs. Others are predominantly social groupings of general and specialty contractors who meet occasionally in one another's homes to share information and camaraderie on an informal basis. Most of the associations, however, are formally organized as nonprofit corporations with job-procurement and technical-assistance programs. Although most associations operate without benefit of regular paid staff personnel, some local groups with outside funding have staffs as large as 26 people.

Membership in these associations is generally open to contractors of any ethnic or racial background; in fact, some even have a few white members. However, in practice, one racial or ethnic group seems to predominate in each group; in cities where minority contractors of different ethnic or racial backgrounds exist in sufficient numbers, they are organized in separate associations. Thus, for example, in San Francisco, there was a black association, a Latin association, and an Asian-American association. Similarly, black and Spanish-surnamed contractors were organized in separate associations in Denver, Chicago, Houston, Dallas, Los Angeles, and Miami. In several of these cities, such as Houston and Miami, there seemed to be little or no contact between the groups; however, in Los Angeles, the two groups had a good working relationship. Only in San Antonio (where Mexican-Americans and blacks were in the same association) and in New York City (where Puerto Ricans and blacks were members of the same association) have separate ethnic or racial groups organized together in substantial numbers.

FUNDING

Most of the associations are supported, at least in part, by membership dues and fees charged for providing such services as estimating or bond packaging. However, because the member firms are typically small and undercapitalized themselves, monies from these sources are insufficient to support staff salaries and other expenses essential to maintain programs of job procurement and technical assistance. Two exceptions were the Brotherhood of Minority Contractors in New York City and the Central Contractors

Association of Seattle, whose spokespersons reported that their programs are operated entirely by membership support. Some groups survived on the contributions of staff time and office space volunteered by their more established member-contractor firms. Others, such as General and Specialty Contractors Association of Oakland and the Polk County Minority Contractors Association of Lake Wales, Florida, obtained free office space in housing management offices for housing projects which their membership helped to sponsor through third-party organizations.

Most funding for local associations, however, has come in grants from government and foundation sources, including the Ford Foundation, the OMBE, the Economic Development Administration, the Department of Labor, and local Model Cities programs. In addition, five national insurance companies lent $5 million through the MCAP in Washington, D. C. , to local associations to establish revolving loan funds for minority contractors. Although precise information on how much outside funding had been provided to local minority contractor associations through 1975 is unavailable, a good educated guess would be 14 to 18 million dollars. Probably the largest source of funding has been grants from local Model Cities programs, which became defunct in the mid-1970s. Most of the funding to minority contractor associations was earmarked to provide minority firms with specific services such as loan or bonding packaging, a revolving loan fund, technical assistance, or labor training.

FUNCTIONS

Local minority contractors' associations have operated with a variety of approaches to assist their individual members.

First, they bring minority firms into contact with the mainstream construction industry by generally making the contractors more visible.

They help minority firms locate and secure jobs by serving as a clearinghouse to gather information on upcoming jobs from such informal sources as personal contacts as well as such formal sources as the Dodge Reports; by serving an outreach function for white general contractors who want to work with qualified minority contractors; by getting names of their members placed on select bidders lists of private and public agencies; by negotiating to ensure that at least portions of the work on larger government projects go to minority firms—either as prime general or subcontractors, third-tier subcontractors, or joint-venture partners; and by helping contractors to prequalify for the 8(a) program of the SBA.

They educate and offer managerial and technical assistance to minority firms to enable them to better operate their businesses by helping them improve their accounting systems; providing assistance with bidding and estimation; loan packaging and teaching contractors the procedures involved in obtaining loans; surety bond packaging and teaching contractors bonding procedures involved; encouraging journeymen to become qualified to start their own firms and helping them become properly established in the beginning with such matters as licensing and tax registration; and helping minority contractors negotiate joint ventures.

They help focus community resources on their membership by prodding government agencies to better implement programs authorized by Congress; administering labor training programs for member contractors and providing the institutional component of the programs; administering revolving loan funds; and bringing contractors into touch with community experts from local universities, contractors' associations, and professional associations to advise and tutor individual contractors and to speak at association meetings.

They act as spokespersons and representatives of busy contractors who are beset by special problems on the job. For example, they act as ombudsmen to help contractors involved in dealing with governmental assistance programs and in performing government work (especially for the first time); they negotiate with union representatives over tough labor-management issues on the job, and with general contractors or owners to stop harrassment by an individual racist superintendent or fellow subcontractor on the job.

They provide various useful services to contractors, such as making available an office center with secretarial and bookkeeping services; helping member contractors to compete with larger contractors by arranging to buy materials in bulk or equipment at discount; providing information to contractors on matters of concern to their businesses, such as new technological or legal developments, for example, the Williams-Steiger Occupational Health and Safety Act of 1970; and buying commonly used specialized construction equipment and renting it at below-market rates.

Examining this list of functions, one might legitimately ask if many of these tasks could not be performed by a general minority business-development center rather than specialized minority contractor associations. It is certainly theoretically possible that general business-development centers could handle some of the functions. However, because such centers generally lack staff with construction expertise, they are unlikely to perform effectively. Construction is a unique industry that requires a specialized approach. Further, there is potential for developing minority enterprise in construction sufficient to warrant a specialized approach. Contract construction is one of the largest industrial sectors in the United States, and more than one out of every ten existing minority firms in 1972 were construction contractors.

Of all the functions in which minority contractor associations have engaged, they have been best at procuring jobs. Helping the contractor to perform these jobs successfully with managerial and technical assistance is more difficult. In part, this difficulty arises because of the inability of many minority associations to attract and hold technically competent staff, owing to uncertainty about future continuity of funding.

VIEWS OF MEMBERSHIP

Minority contractors interviewed generally seemed pleased with the performance of their associations. In fact, contractors seemed to view the government-supported associations more favorably than any other government program to upgrade minority enterprise.

However, the associations did not have the universal approval of the contractors interviewed. From the tone and content of the comments made in the interviews, it is readily apparent that some contractors greet any assistance effort aimed at them with skepticism. In part, this skepticism is a legacy of broken promises in the past.

Many of the negative comments centered on politics within the associations, especially from respondents who felt they were not getting sufficient assistance. Although the functions of the organizations may be strictly technical, decisions regarding allocation of effort can be highly political. Such a situation has been common in other government assistance efforts to businesses (for example, the agricultural extension service) and indeed is difficult to avoid. In order to generate a successful record worthy of refunding, an association will naturally tend to focus efforts on firms they judge have the most potential for success. Such an allocation is likely to upset weaker contractors who think they have just as much potential as the recipients of the assistance.

In practice, allocation decisions seem to be made roughly according to ability and to the degree of participation and support individual members provide the association. There are surprisingly few squabbles over particular contracts and assistance efforts when they are offered. Concern among the contractors seems to arise ex post facto when the members notice that the firm of an association official or someone close to the executive director has enjoyed more than its proportionate share of assistance.

It would be difficult—if not impossible—to establish hard and fast rules and procedures regarding allocation of assistance. In the absence of such rules and procedures, some abuses stemming from outright favoritism are bound to occur. In view of this, it would perhaps be useful for sponsoring agencies to establish some sort of appeals procedure for contractors who feel they have been abused.

CONCLUSIONS

Although minority contractor associations possess vast potential for advancing minority enterprise in construction, they are not without problems and shortcomings. Like any human institution, individual associations are subject to human problems such as weak or domineering or ill-motivated leadership, political infighting among members of the organization (often over charges of favoritism in the allocation of jobs or assistance), personality conflicts, fragmentation of contractor groups, and lack of foresight in neglecting long-range planning.

In the long run, the planning problem is connected with the funding problem of minority contractor associations. As one official from a minority contractor association in Texas stated: "You want me to make long-range plans? You assure me of funding for five years—then I'll show you my five-year plan." Regarding the funding issue, some contend that it is unrealistic to expect undercapitalized minority contractors to finance their own organizations. They argue for permanent or very long-run (ten years or more) subsidies from outside sources. Perhaps such funding is needed; but the issue ought to be squarely faced by both contractors and funding agents. While minority contractor associations have tenaciously existed through lean years as well as funded periods, their membership services have been discontinuous and their ability to attract and hold technically competent staff has been hindered.

The importance of access to technically competent staff resources should not be underrated. Long-run technical and managerial proficiency—whether it come from white or black experts, whether they be on the association staff, available as individual volunteers, on loan from established construction firms, or accessible through joint-venture arrangements—seems to be a key element in building minority success stories in construction.

Some of the problems associations face are structural. For example, associations can be of immense help to the small, beginning contractor because they are at present geared to helping the little guy. But what can associations do for larger, established minority contractors to maintain the much-needed support of these "bigger brothers"? Second, how can associations maintain funding adequate to support needed programs from dues and fees collected from their membership when the primary problem facing members is lack of capital? Third, how can associations, which respond to every minority contractor seeking assistance, focus their resources and efforts to help build firms that have the potential for breaking into the large commercial work in the mainstream construction industry? That is, how can they focus their resources on promising firms without suffering charges of favoritism? A fourth structural problem arises from a possible conflict between the two objectives of the associations: developing new contractors and assisting existing firms. Specifically, how can an association avoid assisting journeymen to become contractors in trades already overpopulated with minority firms? For if this happens, the association will have worsened the position of minority firms by merely intensifying competition in marginal construction work.

Many of these problems are growing pains—the sort of problems that any organization faces in pioneering a new effort. But they must be confronted squarely if minority contractors' associations are to achieve their full potential in building minority enterprise in construction. Local minority contractors' associations must learn and grow from the successes and failures of fellow groups around the country. It is a constant and difficult task, but the possible rewards for minority builders—both contractors and workers—are great.

NOTES

1.   The results of the survey are on file at the Center for the Study of Human Resources, University of Texas at Austin. All information compiled was forwarded to the National Minority Business Campaign, Minneapolis, Minnesota, who include a listing of minority contractor associations in their annually published directory of minority business enterprise, Try Us.

2.   More than 70 nationwide associations of construction contractors are listed in 1973 National Trade and Professional Associations and Labor Unions of the United States ed. Craig Colgate, Jr. (Washington, D. C.: Columbia Books, 1973). And this listing is only a partial one, since it omits all independent local and regional associations.

7

CONCLUSIONS AND RECOMMENDATIONS

It is clear that not all minority contractors have the ability and desire to be upgraded. However, some have significant potential for advancement which could be realized with the proper assistance.

This book has reviewed a wide range of efforts designed to assist the advancement of minority contractors. Generally, such efforts can be classified under three rubrics: (1) demand stimulation, (2) supply development, and (3) some combination of the two, such as the joint venture and the minority contractor association.

The first approach examined was demand stimulation through identifying minority firms in published listings. This approach seems to be reasonable, given that minority contractors are out of the mainstream and do not have high visibility. However, identifying firms should be recognized as only a limited first step toward upgrading. Published listings have many inherent limitations and do not ensure that minority firms obtain more work (or even that they are considered for more work). They are a first step and may be helpful, if utilized.

The second approach to demand stimulation considered was directing government contracts at minority firms. Although the federal government lacks a general mandate to promote minority enterprise counterpart to Executive Order 11246 for minority employment, a variety of affirmative-action and set-aside programs has been undertaken by various agencies. Such efforts help to explain why the business volumes of larger minority firms (with ten or more employees) interviewed in Chicago and San Francisco grew substantially from 1969 to 1972.

Unfortunately, however, this group includes few minority firms. Others, constrained by bonding, financial, and performance-capacity problems, did not enjoy such a record.

Supply-development efforts—delivering bonding and financial assistance, managerial and technical help, and labor training—have all been attempted to increase minority contractor capabilities, with mixed results.

The pressure for developing minority firms in construction has come primarily from the federal government, at the prodding of minority contractors themselves. Efforts of private surety companies and banks, while helpful to a few contractors, cannot have widespread effect.

Certainly government assistance to minority enterprise should not offer any ideological or philosophical barrier to consistent thinkers who have agreed with government policies toward business promotion over the past 200 years. Few businesses in this nation have grown to be the giants they are without some special direct or indirect government subsidy. Government assistance has taken various forms: land grants (to railroads), subsidies and technical assistance through extension activities (to farmers), government contracts, direct loans (to Lockheed, for example), tax concessions (to the oil industry and others), protective tariffs, or special legal status (regarding access to minerals in the coal industry). In all these cases, the aim pursued was the good of society. In many, the specific objective has been to maintain employment in a major industry. One can offer similar arguments in favor of promoting minority enterprise in construction.

The problem of upgrading minority contractors has both demand and supply aspects, and both must be encompassed in a remedy. Two vehicles that offer promise in ideally combining both demand stimulation and supply development into one remedy are the joint venture and the minority contractor association. However, the experience to date with the joint venture and the minority contractor association shows that fashioning a remedy is more complex than it appears conceptually; what works in theory has shortcomings and pitfalls in practice. Minority contractor associations face problems of internal politics, personality conflicts, fragmentation of contractor groups, and neglect of long-range planning. Joint ventures between black and white contractors—totally absent in Houston and Atlanta in 1971—abound in San Francisco and Chicago. Yet many joint ventures do not advance the minority contractor. They are for show only—lacking any transfer of performance capability or training.

At least part of the problem involves the still-shaky structures of the minority contractor association and the joint venture.

Minority contractor associations seem to develop, thrive, and grow dormant in response to the availability of outside funding. Joint ventures often develop through negotiation between parties primarily over the basis of how much the nonminority party is willing to concede and how much the minority party is content to accept. Only occasionally the issue of designing the relationship to maximize training and capacity-increasing aspects for the minority contractor is considered.

Characteristics of effective minority contractor associations and meaningful joint-venture arrangements are outlined in the body of this study. Further research along these lines would be productive.

This study shows the need for better monitoring and evaluation procedures for minority contractor associations by funding agencies. Such monitoring should include fiscal as well as performance aspects of the projects. Also, data gathered in monitoring need to be improved. As a specific example, the Concentrated Employment Program in Oakland, which monitored Project UPGRADE, collected only figures on total number of construction placements made—without respect to trade. Since minority participation varies considerably by construction trade, records should be kept by trade. For instance, a placement as an electrician or sheet-metal worker—where few minorities are—would be more of an accomplishment than placement as a plasterer or dry-wall mechanic.

The minority contractors' association can help upgrade its members in several ways. It can help generate access to job opportunities for minority contractors as well as assisting them to take advantage of the opportunities, thereby dealing with both the demand and supply aspects of the problem. As the experiences of minority contractors' associations in Oakland, Los Angeles, and elsewhere have demonstrated, the association approach can be especially useful in dealing with the financial and bonding problems of contractors. Further assistance has been provided with the programs for bonding guarantees and interim financing recently initiated by the SBA.

Associations of minority contractors have been keenly aware of a need for labor training. As revealed in the interviews, few minority firms currently operate formal labor training programs. However, several contractors expressed a willingness to participate in a government-sponsored labor training effort, "given the proper sort of program." According to the contractors interviewed, if the federal government were to offer a training program to minority contractors, it should be operated through a minority contractors' association. The association approach offers advantages over contracting with individual firms for several reasons. First, the association could probably better handle the administrative details.

Second, the association would be in a better position to provide supportive services and an institutional training component for the trainees. Third, if the training contract were solely with an individual firm, the trainee would be required to work for that firm only. Such an arrangement would cause difficulties, since most minority-owned firms are small and have unsteady work. If the contract were arranged with a consortium of firms, the trainee could work for several enterprises, thus assuring him of more steady work and better exposure to a variety of work experience.

Admittedly, significant problems can arise in funding minority contractor associations to perform labor training. Experience with past programs has revealed that special problems occur when the labor training contract is the sole source of financial support available to the association. In such cases, associations naturally attempt to utilize the labor training funds to fulfill a variety of administrative and other association needs, thereby diluting the quantity and quality of the labor training performed.

By itself, upgrading minority contractors does not offer a shortcut solution to achieving integration in the building-trades unions. However, it is one of several routes that can be profitably pursued to accomplish this aim. If minority firms could be upgraded to a level where they became a significant bloc of the industry, white institutions such as unions and contractors' associations could not afford to ignore them. However, it should be recognized that, at least for the immediate future, potential for achieving integration of the trades in this manner is quite limited, because in trades in which the unions have fewest minority members, minority contractors are generally scarce, too; minority contractors currently employ under 10 percent of the minority work force in construction; although three-quarters of the southern minority contractors surveyed want to expand their businesses, only a fourth of these firms aspire to work in the unionized (large commercial and industrial construction) sectors; and the larger a minority construction firm grows, the smaller the proportion of minority workers it tends to employ.

It should be added, however, that according to the available evidence, minority enterprise in construction seems to have relatively greater employment-generating potential than other industries.[1] Further, the strength of minority firms varies substantially by place and trade.

A few minority firms currently operate under union contract, and, if upgraded, many others would not be averse to signing a union contract. However, the result would not be significant enough in itself to integrate the trades. Other approaches must be tried, such as meaningful legal and administrative pressure for affirmative action and apprenticeship outreach to place minority youngsters into apprenticeship.

In fact, the importance of promoting black participation in apprenticeship programs is underscored by the results of this study. In the South, black colleges such as Tuskegee Institute have been a primary source of training for past and present black contractors, especially in the mechanical trades. However, recent revisions in curriculum have eliminated the programs that produced these entrepreneurs. If blacks are to be represented among mechanical trade contractors in the future, the apprenticeship training programs that have provided training to significant proportions of Anglo contractors must also be available to minorities—especially in the South.

Since the upgrading potential of many minority construction firms hinges on the ability to employ capable middle managers and field superintendents, the need for minorities qualified through training is even more immediate and pronounced.

Another important potential source of training that needs greater minority participation is the courses and programs on construction technology currently offered in 83 colleges and universities across the nation.[2] To provide a pool of qualified minority superintendents and middle managers, as well as a potential pool of future minority contractors, greater emphasis should be placed on affirmative action in the construction programs of institutions of higher education.

In addition to federal agencies and minority contractors' associations, other parties can assist in upgrading the minority contractor, including white contractors, white consumers, local government agencies, labor unions, and the surety and finance industries.

Individual white contractors could assist minority contractors by engaging in meaningful joint-venture relationships with minority contractors, seeking to utilize more minority subcontractors, and offering minority contractors technical assistance. An additional effort would be to provide consulting services to minority contractors for dealing with problems in such areas as bidding and estimating or accounting or to provide minority contractors with introductions to bonding agents and banking officials.

White consumers can play a role in helping the minority contractors to break into white building markets. In relying on minority community institutions alone, black and Mexican-American contractors face the danger of having their businesses confined to a minority market. White institutional consumers, such as churches and universities, could lead the way in helping minorities to break into white markets for larger construction jobs. For example, efforts such as Project Equality, an interdenominational church program aimed at equal employment opportunity, could be expanded to ensure that not only minority workers but also minority contractors and subcontractors participate in church construction and the numerous construction projects built under the sponsorship of its member churches.[3] Likewise, white universities might become responsive to the issue.[4] Individual white consumers also can help provide minority contractors with work by negotiating construction contracts directly with minority contractors or subcontractors instead of letting the contracts for open bidding, by requiring or encouraging prime contractors to utilize minority subcontractors, or simply by ensuring that minorities are invited to bid and that their bids are seriously considered.

Local governments can also play a role in facilitating the advancement of the minority contractor. As noted earlier, minority contractors interviewed expressed a greater interest in state and local government construction than any other type of government work. However, information on state and local government construction opportunities is not readily accessible to contractors. A 1970 survey made by Sam Sperling of the City of Los Angeles Office of Contract Compliance found a total of 230 separate government agencies issuing contracts to bid in the Los Angeles area alone—each with its own procedure for publishing such information.[5] Faced with a bewildering variety of notification procedures, a minority contractor might understandably soon give up any ideas about performing government construction work. To correct this situation, a local government agency might compile a list of notification procedures used by various government agencies within the locality. (Sperling compiled such information for Los Angeles.) Such a project not only would benefit interested minority contractors but also could have the salutary effect of reducing construction costs to government agencies involved by increasing competition.

Further, state and local governments can follow the lead of the federal government in directing more of their procurement to minority firms. Many local governments have already begun this effort. The UDC of New York State started a program that combined demand stimulation and supply development in one program.[6] Illinois passed an Illinois Small Business Purchasing Act which in effect established the office of ombudsman to help small businesses increase their participation in state contracts.[7] Further efforts need to be made to assure affirmative action in utilizing minority contractors on state and local work, particularly as the use of revenue sharing increases.

From the point of view of public officials, encouraging minority contractors to bid may bring some definite benefits. By injecting a fresh element of competition into government procurement, often longstanding "sweetheart" alliances between agency and supplier are unsettled with beneficial results to taxpayers. Procurement officials in Los Angeles and Illinois interviewed for the study pointed to examples of sharp reduction in price on new contracts with minority contractors in the bidder's circle. While some of these low prices are admittedly due to either submission of an impossibly low bid by the minority, or to temporary below-competitive pricing by existing nonminority suppliers aimed at driving out competition, most of the cases were described as simply matters of long-overdue shakeups in traditional bidding arrangements. [8]

Specific local agencies could also assist the upgrading effort. For example, especially in the South, the local vocational-education agency could play a key role in helping minority contractors combat their labor problem by working in conjunction with a minority contractors' association. Perhaps a cooperative work-study program could be arranged, or at least a better placement program for vocational-program graduates in construction could be coordinated.

Labor unions can take some positive steps to assist minority contractors. As noted previously, a major reason why contractors avoid signing union contracts is fear of low-quality jobs. At least one labor union in Atlanta has attempted to resolve this problem by helping to ensure that its newly signed minority contractors are considered for good projects.

The surety industry—especially at the local level—can also do more to assist minority contractors. Surety agents can establish relationships with associations of minority contractors and can help educate members in procedures used by the industry. Further, the industry can eliminate misunderstanding by revealing the reasons why bonding applications of minority contractors have been denied.

Banks can likewise establish working relationships with minority contractors' associations to help contractors with their financial problems and can agree to participate in the new SBA program for interim financing. Further, they can expand the capacity of a revolving loan fund by agreeing to lend a multiple of the fund monies deposited with them. Perhaps most importantly, they can improve upon their affirmative-action efforts to increase the number of minority loan officers, to whom many minority contractors feel they can best relate, to overcome what they observe to be the most pressing problem—lack of financing.

In summary, though it is unwise to expect grandiose results from efforts to upgrade the few existing minority contractors, there is some limited, realizable potential for improving and expanding minority business in construction. Several agencies and groups can play a role in this effort; but the existence of strong minority contractors' associations is probably central to almost any successful endeavor.

NOTES

1.   Timothy Bates, "Employment Potential of Inner City Black Enterprise," The Review of Black Political Economy 4 (Summer 1974): 65.

2.   A listing of schools of higher education offering construction curricula is provided in Construction Education Directory 2d. ed. (Washington, D.C.: The Associated General Contractors of America, Education and Research Foundation, 1974).

3.   A description of Project Equality can be found in Michael Stone, "Project Equality Today: A Case Study of the Church in the Social Order," The Christian Century, January 21, 1970, pp. 79-82.

4.   For detailed recommendations on the issue of participation of minorities in university construction, see Howard E. Mitchell, Marion B. Fox, and James S. Roberts, "A Report to President Gaylord P. Harnwell on the University of Pennsylvania Employment Policy in the Construction Trades" (Philadelphia: Minority Employment Project, University of Pennsylvania, 1969). On page 62, it is recommended that nonwhite subcontractors and contractors be awarded contracts on University of Pennsylvania building sites.

5.   Personal interview with Sam Sperling, Office of Contract Compliance, City of Los Angeles, December 24, 1970.

6.   Telephone interview with Donald Coesville, affirmative-action officer, UDC, New York City, August 2, 1973.

7.   Telephone interview with William Gray, coordinator for small business procurement, Illinois State Department of General Services, Springfield, Ill., May 17, 1974.

8.   Confidential communication, 1973.

APPENDIX: TABLES DETAILING INFORMATION COLLECTED IN INTERVIEWS WITH CONSTRUCTION CONTRACTORS

TABLE A.1

Contractors Interviewed, by Current Age:
By City and Racial/Ethnic Background

	25 or under	26-30	31-35	36-40	41-45	46-50	51-55	56-60	61-65	66 or over	Mean Average Age	Total Respondents
Atlanta												
Black	—	3	5	11	7	9	6	3	5	1	45.4	50
Houston												
Black	—	2	1	3	—	2	3	—	—	—	41.5	11
Spanish-American	1	5	7	16	10	3	5	—	—	—	39.5	47
TOTAL	1	7	8	19	10	5	8	—	—	—	39.9	58
SUBTOTAL, Cities in South	1	10	13	30	17	14	14	3	5	1	42.5	108
Chicago												
Black	3	2	2	5	3	2	5	3	—	1	42.9	26
Spanish-American	—	—	2	4	3	3	2	—	—	—	43.1	14
TOTAL	3	2	4	9	6	5	7	3	—	1	42.9	40
San Francisco-Oakland												
Black	—	3	7	13	6	19	21	12	7	1	48.2	89
Spanish-American	—	—	1	3	6	5	5	2	1	1	47.8	24
Spaniard-American	—	—	—	1	—	4	1	1	1	—	48.9	7
Chinese-American	—	—	3	2	3	7	1	1	1	—	44.9	18
Japanese-American	—	—	1	—	1	3	1	—	—	—	46.0	6
American Indian	—	—	—	—	—	1	—	—	1	—	56.5	2
TOTAL	—	3	12	19	16	39	29	15	11	2	47.8	146
SUBTOTAL, Cities in non-South	3	5	16	28	22	44	36	18	11	3	46.7	186
TOTAL MINORITIES, All Cities	4	15	29	58	39	58	50	21	16	4	45.1	294
San Francisco-Oakland												
White	—	—	1	1	2	7	3	3	2	4	53.6	23

Source: Personal interviews with contractors. Data for Atlanta and Houston were gathered in 1971. Data for Chicago and San Francisco-Oakland were collected during 1973-74.

TABLE A.2

Contractors Interviewed, by Age at Founding of Firm:
By City and Racial/Ethnic Background

	Age Categories									Mean Average Age at Founding of Firm	Total Respondents
	25 or under	26–30	31–35	36–40	41–45	46–50	51–55	56–60	61 or more		
Atlanta											
Black	11	8	11	9	4	5	1	—	—	33.3	49
Houston											
Black	5	3	3	—	—	—	—	—	—	26.5	11
Spanish-American	10	14	7	9	4	2	1	—	—	31.9	47
TOTAL	15	17	10	9	4	2	1	—	—	30.9	58
SUBTOTAL, Cities in South	26	25	21	18	8	7	2	—	—	32.0	107
Chicago											
Black	3	7	5	6	3	1	1	—	—	34.5	26
Spanish-American	1	1	6	3	3	1	1	—	—	37.1	16
TOTAL	4	8	11	9	6	2	2	—	—	35.5	42
San Francisco-Oakland											
Black	7	15	27	11	16	10	2	1	—	36.2	89
Spanish-American	1	3	3	6	5	2	2	1	—	39.4	23
Spaniard-American	—	1	5	—	1	—	—	—	—	34.0	7
Chinese-American	3	3	6	6	—	—	—	—	—	32.3	18
Japanese-American	—	1	5	—	—	—	—	—	—	31.3	6
American Indian	—	—	2	—	—	—	—	—	—	34.0	2
TOTAL	11	23	48	23	22	12	4	2	—	35.9	145
SUBTOTAL, Cities in non-South	15	31	59	32	28	14	6	2	—	35.8	187
TOTAL MINORITIES, All Cities	41	56	80	50	36	21	8	2	—	34.4	294
San Francisco-Oakland											
Whites	5	7	2	1	4	3	8	1	—	34.7	23

Source: Personal interviews with contractors. Data for Atlanta and Houston were gathered in 1971. Data for Chicago and San Francisco-Oakland were collected during 1973-74.

123

TABLE A.3

Contractors Interviewed, by Grade Level, Formal
Education: By City and Racial/Ethnic Background

	Grade Level Formal Education								Total Responses	Mean Grade Level Completed
	0	1-4	5-8	9-11	12	13-15	16	17 and above		
Atlanta										
Black	0	3	4	10	13	10	8	2	50	12.0
Houston										
Black	0	0	2	0	1	4	6	0	13	13.7
Spanish-American[a]	2	6	14	10	7[b]	5	4	1	49	9.1
Chicago										
Black	0	1	1	6	7	9	2	0	26	11.9
Spanish-American	0	0	6	2	2	4	0	1	15	10.6
San Francisco-Oakland										
Black	0	3	12	16	34	14	10	2	91	11.5
Spanish-American	0	0	8	2	7	5	3	0	25	11.0
Spaniard-American	0	0	1	2	0	4	1	0	8	12.0
Chinese-American	0	0	2	3	3	7	2	1	18	12.4
Japanese-American	0	0	0	0	0	0	2	4	6	15.2
American Indian	0	0	0	0	2	0	0	0	2	12.0
White	0	1	1	1	11	6	4	1	25	12.9

[a]Five contractors completed their schooling in Mexico. The Mexican grade-level system differs a little from the one used in the United States, so the grade levels were converted into U.S. equivalents for the purposes of analysis.

[b]Four of the seven high school diplomas were earned by taking the GED examination.

Source: Personal interviews with contractors. Data for Atlanta and Houston were gathered in 1971. Data for Chicago and San Francisco-Oakland were collected during 1973-74.

Contractors Interviewed, by Business Background:
By City and Racial/Ethnic Background

	Both Business Training and Previous Business Experience	Business Training Only	Previous Business Experience Only	Neither Business Training nor Business Experience	Total Responses
Atlanta					
Black	5	6	7	24	42
Houston					
Black	3	3	1	4	11
Spanish-American	5	6	10	30	51
TOTAL	8	9	11	34	62
TOTAL, Cities in South	13	15	18	58	104
Chicago					
Black	6	7	6	7	26
Spanish-American	—	2	2	11	15
TOTAL	6	9	8	18	41
San Francisco-Oakland					
Black	13	18	18	43	92
Spanish-American	2	4	8	11	25
Spaniard-American	1	—	1	6	8
Chinese American	—	4	3	11	18
Japanese-American	—	1	1	4	6
American Indian	—	—	1	1	2
TOTAL	16	27	32	76	151
TOTAL, Cities in non-South	22	36	40	94	192
TOTAL, All Cities	35	51	58	152	296

Source: Personal interviews with minority contractors. Data for Atlanta and Houston were gathered in 1971.
Data for Chicago and San Francisco-Oakland were collected during 1973-74.

TABLE A.5

Contractors Interviewed, by Original Trade; By City and Racial/Ethnic Background

	Air-Conditioning/ Heating/ Sheet Metal	Carpentry/ Cabinet Maker/ Drywall Hanger	Concrete	Electrician	Iron-worker	Mason/ Bricklayer	Painter	Plasterer/ Lather	Plumber/ Pipefitter	Roofer	Tile-setter/ Terrazzo	Other	Unspecified	No Trade	Total Responses
Atlanta															
Black	6	12	—	3	1	12	3	2	4	1	2	3	—	3	52
Houston															
Black	1	6	1	1	—	1	1	—	2	1	—	—	—	—	13
Spanish-American	6	12	—	2	—	—	2	—	6	1	10	5	—	7	51
TOTAL	7	18	1	3	—	1	3	—	8	2	10	5	—	7	64
SUBTOTAL, Cities in South	13	30	1	6	1	13	6	2	12	3	12	8	—	10	116
Chicago															
Black	3	2	1	1	1	1	—	2	5	—	1	4	2	4	27
Spanish-American	—	4	—	3	—	1	—	—	2	—	—	1	—	4	15
TOTAL	3	6	1	4	1	2	—	2	7	—	1	5	2	8	42
San Francisco-Oakland															
Black	1	27	4	5	1	1	15	5	10	2	2	7	1	7	91
Spanish-American	3	7	—	2	2	2	1	1	1	1	—	2	1	4	25
Spaniard-American	1	1	—	2	—	—	1	—	1	—	—	—	—	—	6
Chinese-American	1	4	—	5	—	—	4	—	—	—	—	—	—	4	18
Japanese-American	—	2	—	—	—	—	—	—	—	—	—	1	—	1	4
American Indian	—	2	—	—	—	—	—	—	—	—	—	—	—	—	2
TOTAL	6	43	4	14	3	3	21	6	12	3	2	10	2	16	146
SUBTOTAL, Cities in non-South	9	49	5	18	4	5	21	8	19	3	3	15	4	24	188
TOTAL MINORITIES, All Cities	22	79	6	24	5	18	27	10	31	6	15	23	4	34	304
San Francisco-Oakland															
White	—	7	—	2	1	2	3	—	1	1	—	1	—	7	25

Source: Personal interviews with contractors. Data for Atlanta and Houston were gathered in 1971. Data for Chicago and San Francisco-Oakland were collected during 1973-74.

126

TABLE A.6

Contractors Interviewed, by Source of Training:
By City, and Racial/Ethnic Background

		Sources of Training						
	"Picked it Up on the Job"	Postsecondary Vocational Education (including Private Vocational Education)	High School Vocational Education	Union Apprenticeship	Federal Government Manpower Program	Armed Forces	Other	Total Respondents*
Atlanta								
Black	22	15	5	6	2	1	—	47
Houston								
Black	10	7	2	—	—	1	—	13
Spanish-American	40	7	4	5	—	—	—	46
TOTAL	50	14	6	5	—	1	—	59
SUBTOTAL, Cities in South	72	29	11	11	2	2	—	106
Chicago								
Black	8	2	2	7	—	—	4	20
Spanish-American	6	3	2	3	—	—	1	14
TOTAL	14	5	4	10	—	—	5	34
San Francisco-Oakland								
Black	54	7	2	26	1	1	2	54
Spanish-American	14	2	—	10	—	1	—	23
Spaniard-American	2	—	—	3	—	1	2	7
Chinese-American	11	3	1	2	—	1	—	17
Japanese-American	4	—	—	—	—	—	1	5
American Indian	—	—	—	2	—	—	1	2
TOTAL	85	12	3	43	1	4	5	108
SUBTOTAL, Cities in non-South	99	17	7	53	1	4	10	142
TOTAL MINORITIES, All Cities	171	46	18	64	3	6	10	248
San Francisco-Oakland								
White	10	2	—	8	—	—	—	23

*The total respondents figure does not necessarily agree with the total number of responses, since a few contractors reported two or more sources.

Source: Personal interview with contractors. Data for Atlanta and Houston were gathered in 1971. Data for Chicago and San Francisco-Oakland were collected during 1973-74.

TABLE A.7

Contractors Interviewed, by Years of Experience at Trade: By City and Racial/Ethnic Background

	Years of Experience at Trade					Mean Average Years at the Trade	Total Respondents
	2 or less	3-5	6-10	11-14	15 or more		
Atlanta							
Black	—	—	2	7	34	24.0	43
Houston							
Black	1	—	2	—	9	23.3	11
Spanish-American	1	1	6	5	32	17.9	45
TOTAL	1	1	8	5	41	19.0	56
SUBTOTAL, Cities in South	1	1	10	12	75	21.2	99
Chicago							
Black	—	1	3	5	14	18.9	23
Spanish-American	2	1	2	1	8	15.4	14
TOTAL	2	2	5	6	22	17.6	37
San Francisco-Oakland							
Black	1	1	4	8	69	23.5	83
Spanish-American	—	1	1	2	20	22.0	24
Spaniard-American	—	—	—	—	7	29.0	7
Chinese-American	—	1	1	3	12	19.5	17
Japanese-American	—	—	—	—	5	20.0	5
American Indian	—	—	—	—	2	37.0	2
TOTAL	1	3	6	13	115	23.1	138
SUBTOTAL, Cities in non-South	3	5	11	19	137	21.9	175
TOTAL MINORITIES, All Cities	4	6	21	31	212	21.7	274
San Francisco-Oakland							
White	1	2	1	1	18	28.4	23

Source: Personal interviews with contractors. Data for Atlanta and Houston were gathered in 1971. Data for Chicago and San Francisco-Oakland were collected during 1973-74.

TABLE A.8

Contractors Interviewed, by Time in Trade Before Going into Business for Self: By City and Racial/Ethnic Background

	Years in Trade Before Becoming Self-employed									Total Respondents
	1 or less	2	3	4	5	6–10	11–15	16–20	21 or more	
Atlanta										
Black	4	3	2	—	4	8	9	7	7	44
Houston										
Black	2	—	—	1	—	5	1	2	—	11
Spanish–American	4	1	1	3	2	13	13	4	3	44
TOTAL	6	1	1	4	2	18	14	6	3	55
SUBTOTAL, Cities in South	10	4	3	4	6	26	23	13	10	99
Chicago										
Black	1	—	2	2	2	7	3	2	4	23
Spanish–American	1	1	1	—	2	4	2	2	1	14
TOTAL	2	1	3	2	4	11	5	4	5	37
San Francisco–Oakland										
Black	3	4	3	4	—	28	20	11	9	82
Spanish–American	1	1	2	—	3	5	4	1	4	21
Spaniard–American	—	—	—	—	—	3	3	—	1	7
Chinese–American	2	1	—	1	1	10	1	1	—	17
Japanese–American	—	—	—	—	—	3	2	—	—	5
American Indian	—	—	—	—	—	—	—	—	2	2
TOTAL	6	6	5	5	4	49	30	13	16	134
SUBTOTAL, Cities in non-South	8	7	8	7	8	60	35	17	21	171
TOTAL MINORITIES, All Cities	18	11	11	11	14	86	58	30	31	270
San Francisco–Oakland										
White	3	1	1	4	2	4	4	1	3	23

Source: Personal interviews with contractors. Data for Atlanta and Houston were gathered in 1971. Data for Chicago and San Francisco–Oakland were collected during 1973–74.

Proportion of Contractors Interviewed with a Relative in Construction:
By City and Racial/Ethnic Background

	Have a Relative in Construction	As a Percent of Total Respondents	Total Respondents
Atlanta			
Black	31	63	49
Houston			
Black	6	50	12
Spanish-American	35	71	49
TOTAL	41	67	61
SUBTOTAL, Cities in South	72	65	110
Chicago			
Black	14	54	26
Spanish-American	10	63	16
TOTAL	24	57	42
San Francisco-Oakland			
Black	45	50	91
Spanish-American	8	32	25
Spaniard-American	3	38	8
Chinese-American	1	6	16
Japanese-American	3	50	6
American Indian	1	50	2
TOTAL	61	41	148
SUBTOTAL, Cities in non-South	85	45	190
TOTAL MINORITIES, All Cities	157	52	300
San Francisco-Oakland			
White	8	32	25

Source: Personal interviews with contractors. Data for Atlanta and Houston were gathered in 1971. Data for Chicago and San Francisco-Oakland were collected during 1973-74.

TABLE A.10

Contractors Interviewed, by Father's Principal Occupation:
By City and Racial/Ethnic Background

	Father's Principal Occupation											
	Self-Employed							Not Self-Employed				
		Construction Contractor										
	Total	Same Trade	Different Trade	Trade Un-specified	Independent Farmer or Rancher	Other Nonconstruction Business	Self Em-ployed Un-specified	Total	Con-struction Employee	Employee, Other than Construction	Employee, Un-specified	Total Re-spondents
Atlanta												
Black	25	7	6	—	8	4	—	22	7	15	—	47
Houston												
Black	9	4	—	—	3	2	—	4	1	3	—	13
Spanish-American	26	5	2	—	12	7	—	22	4	18	—	48
TOTAL	35	9	2	—	15	9	—	26	5	21	—	61
SUBTOTAL												
Cities in South	60	16	8	—	23	10	3	48	12	36	—	108
Chicago												
Black	14	2	4	—	5	3	—	8	1	7	2	24
Spanish-American	10	5	—	—	1	4	—	5	—	5	—	15
TOTAL	24	7	4	—	6	7	—	13	1	12	2	39
San Francisco-Oakland												
Black	31	4	2	2	13	10	—	43	5	37	2	76
Spanish-American	10	2	1	—	3	4	1	11	—	11	—	21
Spaniard-American	6	1	1	—	1	2	—	2	—	2	—	8
Chinese-American	10	—	1	—	—	9	—	7	—	7	1	18
Japanese-American	5	1	—	1	1	3	—	1	—	1	—	6
American Indian	1	—	—	—	—	—	—	1	—	1	—	2
TOTAL	63	8	5	3	18	28	1	65	6	59	3	131
SUBTOTAL												
Cities in non-South	87	15	9	3	24	35	1	78	7	71	—	170
TOTAL MINORITIES												
All Cities	147	31	17	3	47	45	4	131	19	107	5	278
San Francisco-Oakland												
White	14	1	1	3	4	2	3	11	3	8	—	25

Source: Personal interviews with contractors. Data for Atlanta and Houston were gathered in 1971. Data for Chicago and San Francisco-Oakland were collected during 1973–74

131

TABLE A.11

Contractors Interviewed, by Trade Association Membership:
By City and Racial/Ethnic Background

	Minority Trade Association Only	Membership in Construction Trade Associations		None	Total Respondents
		Both Minority and Nonminority Trade Associations	Nonminority Trade Association Only		
Atlanta					
Black	32	9	—	6	50
Houston					
Black	5	3	1	3	12
Spanish-American	18	2	9	21	49
TOTAL	23	5	10	24	61
SUBTOTAL, Cities in South	55	14	10	30	111
Chicago					
Black	18	1	—	6	25
Spanish-American	13	—	—	3	16
TOTAL	31	1	—	9	41
San Francisco-Oakland					
Black	31	20	11	29	91
Spanish-American	13	5	3	4	25
Spaniard-American	2	—	6	—	8
Chinese-American	10	—	—	8	18
Japanese-American	1	—	—	5	6
American Indian	—	—	—	2	2
TOTAL	57	25	20	48	150
SUBTOTAL, Cities in non-South	88	26	20	57	191
TOTAL MINORITIES, All Cities	143	40	30	87	302
San Francisco-Oakland					
White	—	—	15	8	23

Source: Personal interviews with contractors. Data for Atlanta and Houston were gathered in 1971. Data for Chicago and San Francisco-Oakland were collected during 1973-74.

132

TABLE A.12

Contractors Interviewed, by Membership in Construction Unions: By City and Racial/Ethnic Background

Membership in Construction Union	Atlanta Black	Houston Black	Houston Spanish-American	Houston Total	Subtotal, Cities in South	Chicago Black	Chicago Spanish-American	Chicago Total
Never a member	22	7	34	41	63	6	7	12
Yes, a member	23	3	15	18	41	18	11	27
(As a percent of total respondents)	51	30	31	31	39	74	63	69
Mechanical Trades								
Electricians (IBEW)	—	—	—	—	—	—	2	2
Pipe trades (plumbers or pipefitters or boilermakers)	—	—	5	5	5	4	3	7
Ironworkers	—	—	—	—	—	2	1	3
Operating engineers	1	—	—	—	1	1	—	1
Sheet-metal workers	1	—	1	1	2	1	—	1
Others								
Bricklayers	8	—	1	1	9	1	—	1
Carpenters	6	2	3	5	11	2	4	6
Laborers	1	1	—	1	2	1	—	1
Plasterers	2	—	—	—	2	4	1	5
Painters	2	—	3	3	5	1	—	1
Tilesetters	1	—	1	1	2	—	—	—
Carpet layers	1	—	1	1	2	—	—	—
Roofers	—	—	—	—	—	—	—	—
Lathers	—	—	—	—	—	—	—	—
Glass and glazer workers	—	—	—	—	—	—	—	—
TOTAL RESPONDENTS	45	10	49	59	104	24	18	39

| Membership in Construction Union | Black | San Francisco–Oakland | | | | | | Subtotal, Cities in non-South | Total Minorities, All Cities | San Francisco–Oakland White |
		Spanish-American	Spaniard-American	Chinese-American	Japanese-American	American Indian	Total			
Never a member	16	6	2	4	4	—	33	45	108	2
Yes, a member	70	19	6	10	2	2	106	133	174	16
(As a percent of total respondents)	81	72	75	70	3	100	76	75	62	89
Mechanical Trades										
Electricians (IBEW)	7	2	2	4	—	—	15	17	17	2
Pipe trades (plumbers or pipefitters or boilermakers)	5	2	1	1	—	—	9	16	21	1
Ironworkers	—	1	—	—	—	—	1	4	4	1
Operating engineers	5	—	—	—	—	—	5	6	7	1
Sheet-metal workers	1	2	—	—	—	—	4	5	7	—
Others										
Bricklayers	1	—	1	—	—	—	1	2	11	2
Carpenters	21	7	1	3	2	2	36	42	53	7
Laborers	—	1	—	—	—	—	1	2	4	—
Plasterers	11	—	—	—	—	—	11	16	18	—
Painters	15	1	2	2	—	—	20	21	26	2
Tilesetters	2	—	—	—	—	—	2	2	3	—
Carpet layers	—	—	—	—	—	—	—	—	1	—
Roofers	2	1	—	—	—	—	3	3	3	—
Lathers	—	1	—	—	—	—	1	1	1	—
Glass and glazer workers	—	1	—	—	—	—	1	1	1	1
TOTAL RESPONDENTS	86	25	8	14	6	2	139	178	282	18

Source: Personal interviews with contractors. Data for Atlanta and Houston were gathered in 1971. Data for Chicago and San Francisco–Oakland were collected during 1973–74.

TABLE A.13

Contractors Interviewed, by Years of Experience as Contractors: By City and Racial/Ethnic Background

	Years of Experience				Mean Average Years	Total Respondents
	0-2	3-7	8-14	15 or more		
Atlanta						
Black	10	12	13	17	11.7	52
Houston						
Black	2	2	1	8	15.9	13
Spanish-American	16	10	16	8	7.4	50
TOTAL	18	12	17	16	9.1	63
SUBTOTAL, Cities in South	28	24	30	33	10.3	115
Chicago						
Black	9	10	2	6	8.0	27
Spanish-American	5	7	1	3	6.2	16
TOTAL	14	17	3	9	7.4	43
San Francisco–Oakland						
Black	5	32	22	33	12.4	92
Spanish-American	6	5	4	9	9.5	24
Spaniard-American	0	1	4	3	14.8	5
Chinese-American	1	3	9	5	12.6	18
Japanese-American	0	0	2	4	14.7	6
American Indian	0	0	0	2	22.5	2
TOTAL	12	41	41	56	12.3	150
SUBTOTAL, Cities in non-South	26	51	44	65	11.2	193
TOTAL MINORITIES, All Cities	54	74	74	98	10.9	308
San Francisco–Oakland White	2	3	5	15	18.9	25

Source: Personal interviews with contractors. Data for Atlanta and Houston were gathered in 1971. Data for Chicago and San Francisco-Oakland were collected during 1973–74.

TABLE A.14

Contractors Interviewed, by Commitment to Contracting:
By City and Racial/Ethnic Background

| | Have You Ever Worked as a Craftsworker for Another Employer When Business is Slow? | | Total Respondents |
	Yes	No	
Atlanta			
Black	13	30	43
Houston			
Black	6	6	12
Spanish–American	9	34	43
TOTAL	15	40	55
SUBTOTAL,			
Cities in South	28	70	98
Chicago			
Black	5	21	26
Spanish–American	7	10	17
TOTAL	12	31	43
San Francisco–Oakland			
Black	19	69	88
Spanish–American	8	15	23
Spaniard–American	—	8	8
Chinese–American	2	16	18
Japanese–American	—	6	6
American Indian	—	2	2
TOTAL	29	116	145
SUBTOTAL,			
Cities in non-South	41	147	188
TOTAL MINORITIES,			
All Cities	69	217	286
San Francisco–Oakland			
White	4	18	22

Source: Personal interviews with contractors. Data for Atlanta and Houston were gathered in 1971. Data for Chicago and San Francisco-Oakland were collected during 1973–74.

136

TABLE A.15

Contractors Interviewed, by Age of Present Firm:
By City and Racial/Ethnic Background

| | Age of Present Firm (In Years) | | | | | | | | | Total |
	Less than 1	1	2	3	4	5	6–10	11–15	16 or more	Respondents
Atlanta										
Black	5	4	7	3	2	1	11	5	10	48
Houston										
Black	1	1	2	—	1	—	1	1	5	12
Spanish–American	4	3	9	7	2	3	11	7	3	49
TOTAL	5	4	11	7	3	3	12	8	8	61
SUBTOTAL, Cities in South	10	8	18	10	5	4	23	13	18	109
Chicago										
Black	2	4	3	4	2	1	3	1	5	25
Spanish–American	1	1	2	2	1	4	3	1	1	16
TOTAL	3	5	5	6	3	5	6	2	6	41
San Francisco–Oakland										
Black	1	2	3	16	9	3	21	14	21	90
Spanish–American	—	4	4	2	2	1	5	2	5	25
Spaniard–American	—	—	—	1	—	—	1	3	3	8
Chinese–American	9	—	—	—	1	1	—	—	8	18
Japanese–American	—	—	—	—	1	—	—	2	3	6
American Indian	—	—	—	—	—	—	—	1	1	2
TOTAL	10	6	7	19	12	5	27	22	41	149
SUBTOTAL, Cities in non–South	13	11	12	25	15	10	33	24	47	190
TOTAL MINORITIES, All Cities	23	19	30	35	20	14	56	37	65	299
San Francisco–Oakland										
White	—	1	—	—	1	—	3	2	18	25

Source: Personal interviews with contractors. Data for Atlanta and Houston were gathered in 1971. Data for Chicago and San Francisco–Oakland were collected during 1973–74.

TABLE A.16

Contractors Interviewed, by Form of Business Organization: By City and Racial/Ethnic Background

	Form of Business Organization				Total Respondents
	Proprietorship (Owner-operated)	Partnership	Corporation	As a Percent of Total Respondents	
Atlanta					
Black	35	4	12	24	51
Houston					
Black	6	2	4	33	12
Spanish–American	39	4	4	9	47
TOTAL	45	6	8	14	59
SUBTOTAL, Cities in South	80	10	20	18	110
Chicago					
Black	13	—	13	50	26
Spanish–American	11	2	3	19	16
TOTAL	24	2	16	38	42
San Francisco–Oakland					
Black	68	3	16	18	87
Spanish–American	13	6	6	24	25
Spaniard–American	5	—	3	38	8
Chinese–American	13	—	5	28	18
Japanese–American	2	3	1	17	6
American Indian	1	—	1	50	2
TOTAL	102	12	32	22	146
SUBTOTAL, Cities in non-South	126	14	48	26	188
TOTAL MINORITIES, All Cities	206	24	68	23	298
San Francisco–Oakland					
White	6	3	16	64	25

Source: Personal interviews with contractors. Data for Atlanta and Houston were gathered in 1971. Data for Chicago and San Francisco–Oakland were collected during 1973–74.

Contractors Interviewed, by Union Status of Their Firms:
By City and Racial/Ethnic Background

| | Union Status | | | |
	Union Shop	As a Percent of Total Respondents	Nonunion Shop	Total Respondents
Atlanta				
Black	8	16	41	49
Houston				
Black	0	0	12	12
Spanish–American	3	6	44	47
TOTAL	3	5	56	59
SUBTOTAL, Cities in South	11	9	97	118
Chicago				
Black	20	77	6	26
Spanish–American	6	43	8	14
TOTAL	26	65	14	40
San Francisco–Oakland				
Black	68	77	20	88
Spanish–American	19	79	5	24
Spaniard–American	6	75	2	8
Chinese–American	8	47	9	17
Japanese–American	5	83	1	6
American Indian	1	50	1	2
TOTAL	107	74	38	145
SUBTOTAL, Cities in non-South	133	72	52	185
TOTAL MINORITIES, All Cities	144	49	149	293
San Francisco–Oakland				
White	25	100	0	25

Source: Interviews with contractors. Data for Atlanta and Houston were gathered in 1971. Data for Chicago and San Francisco–Oakland were collected during 1973–74.

TABLE A.18

Contractors Interviewed, by Whether or Not They Operate from an Office:
By City and Racial/Ethnic Background

	Work Out of Home (No Office)	As a Percent of Total Respondents	Work Out of Office	Total Respondents
Atlanta				
Black	33	69	15	48
Houston				
Black	10	83	2	12
Spanish-American	34	69	15	49
TOTAL	44	72	17	61
SUBTOTAL, Cities in South	77	71	32	109
Chicago				
Black	13	50	13	26
Spanish-American	12	75	4	16
TOTAL	25	60	17	42
San Francisco–Oakland				
Black	54	60	36	90
Spanish-American	11	44	14	25
Spaniard-American	2	25	6	8
Chinese-American	12	71	5	17
Japanese-American	1	17	5	6
American Indian	1	50	1	2
TOTAL	81	55	67	148
SUBTOTAL, Cities in non-South	106	56	84	190
TOTAL MINORITIES, All Cities	183	61	116	299
San Francisco–Oakland				
White	8	32	17	25

Source: Personal interviews with contractors. Data for Atlanta and Houston were gathered in 1971. Data for Chicago and San Francisco–Oakland were collected during 1973–74.

140

TABLE A.19

Contractors Interviewed, by Form of Contract Used:
By City and Racial/Ethnic Background

	Form of Contract Used					
	Verbal Predominantly	As a Percent of Total Respondents	Both Verbal and Written, About Equally	Both, Proportion not Specified	Written Predominantly	Total Respondents
Atlanta						
Black	4	9	0	0	39	43
Houston						
Black	3	25	0	0	9	12
Spanish-American	12	26	0	0	34	46
TOTAL	15	26	0	0	43	58
SUBTOTAL, Cities in South	19	19	0	0	82	101
Chicago						
Black	1	5	0	1	17	19
Spanish-American	2	14	0	2	10	14
TOTAL	3	9	0	3	27	33
San Francisco-Oakland						
Black	8	9	3	1	73	85
Spanish-American	2	9	0	0	21	23
Spaniard-American	1	12	0	0	7	8
Chinese-American	4	22	3	0	11	18
Japanese-American	2	33	2	0	2	6
American Indian	0	0	0	0	1	1
TOTAL	17	12	8	1	115	141
SUBTOTAL, Cities in non-South	20	12	8	4	142	174
TOTAL MINORITIES, All Cities	39	14	8	4	224	275
San Francisco-Oakland White	2	8	2	3	17	24

Note: In interviews conducted in Atlanta and Houston, contractors were given only two choices—"verbal predominantly" or "written predominantly."

Source: Personal interviews with contractors. Data for Atlanta and Houston were gathered in 1971. Data for Chicago and San Francisco-Oakland were collected during 1973-74.

TABLE A.20

Contractors Interviewed, by Forms of Insurance Carried: By City and Racial/Ethnic Background

	Forms of Insurance Carried				
	Both Liability Insurance and Workers' Compensation	Liability Insurance Only	Workers' Compensation Only	None	Total Respondents
Atlanta					
Black	31	—	1	15	47
Houston					
Black	7	—	—	5	12
Spanish-American	28	2	1	14	45
TOTAL	35	2	1	19	57
SUBTOTAL, Cities in South	66	2	2	34	104
Chicago					
Black	24	—	—	2	26
Spanish-American	10	1	—	6	17
TOTAL	34	1	—	8	43
San Francisco–Oakland					
Black	75	1	2	2	80
Spanish-American	24	—	—	—	24
Spaniard-American	8	—	—	—	8
Chinese-American	18	—	—	—	18
Japanese-American	6	—	—	—	6
American Indian	2	—	—	—	2
TOTAL	133	1	2	2	138
SUBTOTAL, Cities in non-South	167	2	2	10	181
TOTAL MINORITIES, All Cities	233	4	4	44	285

Source: Personal interviews with minority contractors. Data for Atlanta and Houston were gathered in 1971. Data for Chicago and San Francisco–Oakland were collected during 1973–74.

TABLE A.21

Contractors Interviewed, by Bookkeeping Methods:
By City and Racial/Ethnic Background

	Contractor Himself	Wife or Child	Employee, Secretary, or Office Manager	Employee, Book-keeper or Accountant	Book-keeping Service	Outside Account-ant	Outside Certified Public Accountant	Aided by Advice of Minority Contractors	Total Re-sponses
				Bookkeeper					
Atlanta									
Black	12	3	5	6	7	7	13	2	39
Houston									
Black	4	2	3	2	1	0	5	0	10
Spanish-American	9	8	4	1	19	8	8	1	43
TOTAL	13	10	7	3	20	8	13	1	53
SUBTOTAL, Cities in South	25	13	12	9	27	15	26	3	92
Chicago									
Black	5	2	2	4	3	3	6	1	25
Spanish-American	8	4	0	2	0	1	2	1	16
TOTAL	13	6	2	6	3	4	8	1	41
San Francisco–Oakland									
Black	23	19	5	13	14	11	21	4	91
Spanish-American	7	5	1	4	2	2	6	0	24
Spaniard-American	1	2	3	0	0	1	1	0	8
Chinese-American	8	1	0	2	0	3	4	0	18
Japanese-American	2	1	2	0	0	0	3	0	6
American Indian	0	0	2	0	0	0	0	0	2
TOTAL	41	28	13	19	16	17	35	4	149
SUBTOTAL, Cities in non-South	54	34	15	25	19	21	43	5	190
TOTAL MINORITIES, All Cities	79	47	27	34	46	36	69	7	282
San Francisco–Oakland White	4	2	6	9	1	1	10	0	25

Note: The individual columns may not add to total responses because several contractors made use of more than one method for keeping books.

Source: Personal interviews with contractors. Data for Atlanta and Houston were gathered in 1971. Data for Chicago and San Francisco–Oakland were collected during 1973–74.

143

TABLE A.22

Contractors Interviewed, by Type of Work Firm Performs:
By City and Racial/Ethnic Background

	Type of Work Performed						Total Re- spondents
	Residential Only	Residential Predominantly	Both Residential and Commercial/Industrial (About Equally)	Commercial/Industrial Predominantly	Commercial/Industrial Only	Both Residential and Commercial/Industrial, Proportion Not Specified	
Atlanta							
Black	6	29	—	10	2	—	47
Houston							
Black	3	7	—	2	—	—	12
Spanish-American	12	25	—	9	2	—	48
TOTAL	15	32	—	11	2	—	60
SUBTOTAL, Cities in South	21	61	—	21	4	—	107
Chicago							
Black	1	4	5	11	3	3	27
Spanish-American	3	1	3	—	1	8	16
TOTAL	4	5	8	11	4	11	43
San Francisco—Oakland							
Black	14	19	6	4	5	41	89
Spanish-American	2	5	3	5	1	9	25
Spaniard-American	—	3	—	1	1	3	8
Chinese-American	2	4	4	1	2	5	18
Japanese-American	1	1	—	—	—	4	6
American Indian	—	—	—	—	—	2	2
TOTAL	19	32	13	11	9	64	148
SUBTOTAL, Cities in non-South	23	37	21	22	13	75	191
TOTAL MINORITIES, All Cities	44	98	21	43	17	75	298
San Francisco—Oakland							
White	2	4	3	6	7	3	25

Source: Personal interviews with contractors. Data for Atlanta and Houston were gathered in 1971. Data for Chicago and San Francisco-Oakland were collected during 1973-74.

Contractors Interviewed, by Participation in Government Work:
By City and Racial/Ethnic Background

| | Has the Firm Worked on Any Government Jobs? | | | | | | | | | |
| | Yes | | | | | | | | No | |
	Total	As a Per-cent of Total Re-spondents	Federal	As a Per-cent of Total Re-spondents	State	As a Per-cent of Total Re-spondents	Local—City, County, or School Board	As a Per-cent of Total Re-spondents	spondents	Total
Atlanta										
Black	26	54	24	50	0	0	5	10	22	48
Houston										
Black	8	67	4	33	0	0	5	42	4	12
Spanish-American	16	36	14	31	0	0	10	22	29	45
TOTAL	24	42	18	32	0	0	15	26	33	57
SUBTOTAL, Cities in South	50	48	42	40	0	0	20	19	55	105
Chicago										
Black	21	78	12	44	3	11	19	70	6	27
Spanish-American	7	47	6	40	0	0	4	27	8	15
TOTAL	28	67	18	43	3	7	23	55	14	42
San Francisco-Oakland										
Black	83	90	77	84	23	25	48	52	9	92
Spanish-American	21	84	16	64	8	32	13	52	4	25
Spaniard-American	5	62	4	50	1	12	3	25	3	8
Chinese-American	10	56	10	56	1	6	6	33	8	18
Japanese-American	4	67	1	17	2	33	3	50	2	6
American Indian	2	100	1	50	1	50	1	50	0	2
TOTAL	125	83	109	72	36	24	74	49	26	151
SUBTOTAL, Cities in non-South	153	79	127	66	39	20	97	50	40	193
TOTAL MINORITIES, All Cities	203	75	169	62	39	14	117	43	95	298
San Francisco-Oakland										
White	20	80	18	72	14	56	15	60	5	25

Note: Columns are nonadditive because some contractors have performed work for more than one type of government unit.

Source: Personal interviews with contractors. Data for Atlanta and Houston were gathered in 1971. Data for Chicago and San Francisco-Oakland were collected during 1973-74.

TABLE A.24

Contractors Interviewed, by Size of Largest Contract Performed:
By City and Racial/Ethnic Background

	Chicago			San Francisco-Oakland							Total, Cities in non-South	San Francisco-Oakland White
	Black	Spanish-American	Total	Black	Spanish-American	Spaniard-American	Chinese-American	Japanese-American	American Indian	Total		
$ 1,000 or less	—	1	1	5	1	—	—	—	—	6	7	—
1,001–3,000	1	3	4	5	1	—	—	—	—	6	10	—
3,001–5,000	—	—	—	3	2	—	—	—	—	5	5	—
5,001–10,000	3	1	4	8	1	1	1	2	—	13	17	—
10,001–25,000	5	5	10	14	5	1	3	1	—	24	34	2
25,001–50,000	3	—	3	12	1	2	4	—	—	19	22	2
50,001–75,000	—	2	2	7	4	—	1	1	—	13	15	1
75,001–100,000	—	1	1	10	3	—	1	1	—	15	16	1
100,001–200,000	7	1	8	13	4	2	5	—	—	24	32	6
200,001–500,000	1	—	1	10	1	—	1	1	2	15	16	5
500,001–1,000,000	4	1	5	—	—	—	1	—	—	1	6	2
1,000,001 or more	—	—	—	3	—	1	1	—	—	5	5	6
TOTAL RESPONSES	24	15	39	90	23	7	18	6	2	146	185	25

Source: Personal interviews with contractors. Data for Chicago and San Francisco-Oakland were collected during 1973–74.

146

TABLE A.25

Contractors Interviewed, by Comparison of Largest Contract of Career with Largest Government Contract: by City and Racial/Ethnic Background

	Chicago			San Francisco–Oakland							Total, Cities in non-South	San Francisco–Oakland White
	Black American	Spanish-American	Total	Black American	Spanish-American	Spaniard-American	Chinese-American	Japanese-American	American Indian	Total		
Government contract largest (100%)	8	3	11	30	6	—	3	—	1	40	51	3
Government contract — 90–99% of largest	1	—	1	1	—	—	—	—	—	1	2	—
Government contract — 75–89%	3	—	3	5	2	—	—	—	—	7	10	1
Government contract — 50–74%	3	—	3	10	2	2	—	—	—	14	17	2
Government contract — 25–49%	1	1	2	10	2	1	—	—	—	13	15	5
Government contract — 10–24%	2	2	4	11	2	—	3	1	—	17	21	6
Government contract — less than 10%	3	1	4	6	1	—	2	—	—	9	13	2
Total respondents	21	7	28	73	15	3	8	1	1	101	129	19

Source: Personal interviews with contractors. Data for Chicago and San Francisco–Oakland were collected during 1973–74.

TABLE A.26

Contractors Interviewed, by Annual Gross Dollar Volume of Work Performed:
By City and Racial/Ethnic Background

	Gross Dollar Volume								Median Average Gross Dollar Volume	Total Respondents
	25,000 or less	25,001-50,000	50,001-75,000	75,001-100,000	100,001-200,000	200,001-500,000	500,001-1,000,000	More than 1,000,000		
Atlanta, 1970										
Black	18	10	3	5	3	3	1	2	42,000	45
Houston, 1970										
Black	3	1	—	2	1	1	—	1	75,500	9
Spanish-American	18	8	3	4	6	2	1	—	33,500	42
TOTAL	21	9	3	6	7	3	1	1	—	51
SUBTOTAL, Cities in South, 1970	39(40.6%)	19(19.8%)	6(6.3%)	11(11.5%)	10(10.9%)	6(6.3%)	2(2.1%)	3(3.1%)	—	96
Chicago, 1972										
Black	3	—	3	6	1	4	2	1	—	20
Spanish-American	4	1	1	1	1	1	2	—	—	11
TOTAL	7	1	4	7	2	5	4	1	—	31
San Francisco-Oakland, 1972										
Black and American Indian	24	18	9	6	13	12	3	3	—	88
Spanish-American	5	2	1	2	3	2	2	1	—	18
Spaniard-American	2	—	—	1	1	2	—	1	—	7
Chinese-American	3	3	1	2	3	4	2	—	—	18
Japanese-American	1	—	—	—	3	2	—	—	—	6
TOTAL	35	23	11	11	23	22	7	5	—	137
SUBTOTAL, Cities in non-South	42(25.0%)	24(14.3%)	15(8.9%)	18(10.7%)	25(14.9%)	27(16.1%)	11(6.5%)	6(3.6%)	—	168
TOTAL MINORITIES, All Cities	81(30.7%)	43(16.3%)	21(8.0%)	29(11.0%)	35(13.3%)	33(12.5%)	13(4.9%)	9(3.4%)	—	264
San Francisco-Oakland										
White	4	1	1	1	1	1	2	—	—	11

Source: Personal interviews with contractors. Data for Atlanta and Houston were gathered in 1971. Data for Chicago and San Francisco-Oakland were collected during 1973-74.

148

TABLE A.27

Contractors Interviewed, by Number of Employees Currently on the Payroll: By City and Racial/Ethnic Background

	Total Number of Employees Currently on Payrolls					Total Respondents
	0	1-3	4-9	10-49	50 or more	
Atlanta						
Black	6	20	11	9	2	48
Houston						
Black	4	3	3	2	—	12
Spanish-American	9	20	9	6	1	45
TOTAL	13	23	12	8	1	57
SUBTOTAL, Cities in South	19	43	23	17	3	105
Chicago						
Black	2	6	10	7	1	26
Spanish-American	2	7	2	3	—	14
TOTAL	4	13	12	10	1	40
San Francisco-Oakland						
Black	15	36	22	18	—	91
Spanish-American	—	12	5	6	—	23
Spaniard-American		3	3	2	—	8
Chinese-American	3	7	5	3	—	18
Japanese-American	—	2	3	1	—	6
American-Indian	1	—	—	1	—	2
TOTAL	19	60	38	31	—	148
SUBTOTAL, Cities in non-South	23	73	50	41	1	188
TOTAL MINORITIES, All Cities	43	116	73	58	4	293
San Francisco-Oakland						
White	—	3	3	13	4	23

Source: Personal interviews with contractors. Data for Atlanta and Houston were gathered in 1971. Data for Chicago and San Francisco-Oakland were collected during 1973-74.

TABLE A.28

Racial and Ethnic Composition of Work Force Employed by Contractors Interviewed:
By City and Racial/Ethnic Background

	Total Number of Employees Currently on Payroll	Total Number of Minority Persons Working for Firm	As a Percent of Total Employees	Total Respondents
Atlanta				
Black	655	360	55	46
Houston				
Black	53	49	92	8
Spanish-American	303.5	206.0	68	—
TOTAL	356.5	255.0	72	—
SUBTOTAL, Cities in South	1,011.5	617.0	61	—
Chicago				
Black	257	188	73	26
Spanish-American	94	59	64	14
TOTAL	351	247	70	—
San Francisco-Oakland				
Black	507	314	62	91
Spanish-(including Spaniard)American	236	71	30	31
Asian American and American Indian	132	94	71	26
TOTAL	875	479	55	—
SUBTOTAL, Cities in non-South	1,226	726	59	—
TOTAL MINORITIES, All Cities	2,237.5	1,343.0	60	—
Blacks in All Cities	1,472	913	62	—
Spanish-(including Spaniard)Americans, All Cities	633.5	336.0	53	—
Asian-American and American Indian, All Cities	132	94	71	—
San Francisco-Oakland				
Whites	438	133	30	24

Source: Personal interviews with contractors. Data for Atlanta and Houston were gathered in 1971. Data for Chicago and San Francisco-Oakland were collected during 1973-74.

Contractors Interviewed, by Largest Current Source of Financing:
By City and Racial/Ethnic Background

| | Self | As a Percent of Total Respondents | Total | As a Percent of Total Respondents | Financial Institution | | | | | | Total Respondents |
					Minority-owned	Nonminority-owned	Both Minority and Nonminority-owned	Unspecified	SBA	Other	
Atlanta											
Black	27	68	12	30	—	—	1	11	—	1	40
Houston											
Black	6	67	3	33	—	—	—	3	—	—	9
Spanish-American	30	73	4	10	—	2	—	2	—	7	41
TOTAL	36	72	7	14	—	—	—	5	—	7	50
SUBTOTAL, Cities in South	63	70	19	21	—	2	1	16	—	8	90
Chicago											
Black	10	44	11	48	—	10	—	1	1	1	23
Spanish-American	11	85	2	15	—	1	—	1	1	—	13
TOTAL	21	58	13	36	—	11	—	2	2	1	36
San Francisco-Oakland											
Black	38	45	34	41	—	3	—	3	8	5	84
Spanish-American	10	50	9	45	2	6	—	1	—	2	20
Spaniard-American	4	67	2	33	2	2	—	—	—	1	6
Chinese-American	8	50	6	38	2	4	—	—	—	1	16
Japanese-American	2	40	2	40	—	2	—	—	—	—	5
American Indian	1	50	1	50	—	1	—	—	—	—	2
TOTAL	63	47	54	41	4	46	—	4	8	8	133
SUBTOTAL, Cities in non-South	84	50	67	40	4	57	—	6	10	9	169
TOTAL MINORITIES, All Cities	147	57	86	33	4	59	1	22	10	17	259
San-Francisco-Oakland											
White	8	40	12	60	—	5	—	7	—	—	20

Source: Personal interviews with contractors. Data for Atlanta and Houston were gathered in 1971. Data for Chicago and San Francisco-Oakland were collected during 1973-74.

TABLE A.30

Contractors Interviewed, by Experience with Bank Loans:
By City and Racial/Ethnic Background

| | Yes | As a Percent of Total Respondents | Have You Ever Tried to Obtain Bank Loan For Your Business? | | | | Success Rate as a Percent of Total Known Outcome | No | Total |
			With Success	Refused	Outcome Not Stated	In Process			
Atlanta									
Black	30	70	24	6	—	—	56	13	43
Houston									
Black	7	70	7	—	—	—	100	3	10
Spanish-American	25	56	20	4	—	1	83	20	45
TOTAL	32	58	27	4	—	1	87	23	55
SUBTOTAL, Cities in South	62	63	51	10	—	1	84	36	98
Chicago									
Black	24	92	17	3	—	4	85	2	26
Spanish-American	8	53	3	4	1	—	57	7	15
TOTAL	32	78	20	7	1	4	74	9	41
San Francisco-Oakland									
Black	73	82	53	16	4	—	77	16	89
Spanish-American	16	70	10	1	5	—	91	7	23
Spaniard-American	3	38	2	—	1	—	100	5	8
Chinese-American	8	47	6	—	2	—	100	9	17
Japanese-American	3	50	3	—	—	—	100	3	6
American Indian	2	100	2	—	—	—	100	—	2
TOTAL	105	72	76	17	12	—	82	40	145
SUBTOTAL, Cities in non-South	137	74	96	24	13	4	80	49	186
TOTAL MINORITIES, All Cities	199	70	147	34	13	5	81	85	284
San Francisco-Oakland									
White	20	83	12	—	8	—	100	4	24

Source: Personal interviews with contractors. Data for Atlanta and Houston were gathered in 1971. Data for Chicago and San Francisco-Oakland were collected during 1973-74.

152

TABLE A.31

Sources of Labor to Contractors Interviewed:
By City and Racial/Ethnic Background

| | Atlanta | Houston | | | Subtotal, Cities in South |
	Black	Black	Spanish-American	Total	
Informal Sources					
I call employees	12	4	22	26	38
They call me	4	–	8	8	12
Walk-ins—on site or in my office	7	2	8	10	17
Referrals from employees	3	2	2	4	7
Referrals from fellow contractors	4	1	7	8	12
Referrals from suppliers or customers	1	–	6	6	7
Recommendations of friends or relatives	–	1	5	6	6
Hires boys in his neighborhood	–	2	–	2	2
Recruiting trips outside the city	2	1	–	1	3
Shape-ups on street corners	5	–	–	–	5
Formal Sources					
Union or union referral service	6	–	5	5	11
Employment service	7	2	–	2	9
Minority referral organization	–	–	2	2	2
Trade school or training program	5	–	–	–	5
Advertisement in newspaper	2	1	1	2	4
Advertisement on radio or television	1	–	4	4	5
Total respondents	40	11	48	59	99

153

| | San Francisco–Oakland | | | | | | |
Sources	Black	Spanish–American	Spaniard–American	Chinese–American	Japanese–American	American Indian	Total
Informal Sources							
I call employees	27	5	4	7	1	1	45
They call me	22	1	1	1	—	1	26
Walk-ins—on site or in my office	16	1	—	1	—	2	20
Referrals from employees	12	5	2	4	2	1	26
Referrals from fellow contractors	21	8	1	1	2	—	33
Referrals from suppliers or customers	2	—	—	—	—	—	2
Recommendations of friends or relatives	1	—	—	—	—	—	1
Hires boys in his neighborhood	—	—	—	—	—	—	—
Recruiting trips outside the city	—	—	—	—	—	—	—
Shape-ups on street corners	—	—	—	—	—	—	—
Formal Sources							
Union or union referral service	60	13	4	6	3	2	88
Employment service	6	2	2	1	2	—	13
Minority referral organization	2	—	—	2	—	—	4
Trade school or training program	2	—	—	—	—	—	2
Advertisement in newspaper	1	—	—	—	—	—	1
Advertisement on radio or television	—	—	—	—	—	—	—
Total respondents	86	22	8	15	5	2	138

(continued)

154

(Table A.31 continued)

Sources	Chicago			Subtotal, Cities in non–South	Total Minorities, All Cities	San Francisco–Oakland Whites
	Black	Spanish-American	Total			
Informal Sources						
I call employees	13	5	18	63	101	3
They call me	1	2	3	29	41	2
Walk-ins—on site or in my office	2	—	2	22	39	3
Referrals from employees	2	1	3	29	36	1
Referrals from fellow contractors	5	1	6	39	51	5
Referrals from suppliers or customers	1	—	1	3	10	—
Recommendations of friends or relatives	—	—	—	1	7	—
Hires boys in his neighborhood	—	—	—	—	2	—
Recruiting trips outside the city	—	—	—	—	3	—
Shape-ups on street corners	—	—	—	—	5	—
Formal Sources						
Union or union referral service	13	2	15	103	114	19
Employment service	3	—	3	16	25	1
Minority referral organization	—	4	4	8	10	—
Trade school or training program	1	—	1	3	8	—
Advertisement in newspaper	1	1	2	3	7	—
Advertisement on radio or television	—	—	—	—	5	—
Total respondents	26	14	40	178	277	25

Note: The columns add to more than the number of respondents because some of the contractors mentioned more than one source.

Source: Personal interviews with contractors. Data for Atlanta and Houston were gathered in 1971. Data for Chicago and San Francisco–Oakland were collected during 1973–74.

TABLE A.32

Contractors Interviewed, by Whether or Not They Have Trouble Finding and Keeping Reliable and Capable Workers: By City and Racial/Ethnic Background

	Have Trouble	As a Percent of Total Respondents	Have No Trouble	Total Respondents
Atlanta				
Black	28	67	14	42
Houston				
Black	6	67	3	9
Spanish–American	17	42	26	42
TOTAL	23	45	28	51
SUBTOTAL, Cities in South	51	55	42	93
Chicago				
Black	7	29	17	24
Spanish–American	4	29	10	14
TOTAL	11	29	27	38
San Francisco–Oakland				
Black	41	48	44	85
Spanish–American	14	58	10	24
Spaniard–American	1	17	5	6
Chinese–American	11	61	7	18
Japanese–American	3	50	3	6
American Indian	2	100	—	2
TOTAL	72	51	69	141
SUBTOTAL, Cities in non-South	83	46	96	179
TOTAL MINORITIES, All Cities	134	49	138	272
San Francisco–Oakland				
White	8	33	16	24

Source: Personal interviews with contractors. Data for Atlanta and Houston were gathered in 1971. Data for Chicago and San Francisco–Oakland were collected during 1973–74.

TABLE A.33

Contractors Interviewed, by Experience with Bonding: By City and Racial/Ethnic Background

| | Have You Ever Tried to Obtain Bonding? | | | | | As a Percent of | Total |
| | Yes | | | | | | |
	Total	Successful	Refused	Application Pending	No	Total Respondents	Respondents
Atlanta							
Black	20	17	2	1	27	57	47
Houston							
Black	6	3	2	1	5	45	11
Spanish-American	12	5	6	1	35	74	47
TOTAL	18	8	8	2	40	69	58
SUBTOTAL, Cities in South	38	25	10	3	67	64	105
Chicago							
Black	17	12	3	2	10	37	27
Spanish-American	7	6	1	—	9	56	16
TOTAL	24	18	4	2	19	44	43
San Francisco-Oakland							
Black	72	65	3	4	19	21	91
Spanish-American	14	7	3	4	9	39	23
Spaniard-American	6	—	5	1	2	25	8
Chinese-American	12	5	—	7	6	33	18
Japanese-American	4	2	—	2	2	33	6
American Indian	2	—	—	2	—	—	2
TOTAL	120	79	11	20	38	26	148
SUBTOTAL, Cities in non-South	134	97	15	22	57	30	191
TOTAL MINORITIES, All Cities	172	122	25	25	124	42	296
San Francisco-Oakland White	21	18	—	3	1	5	22

Source: Personal interviews with contractors. Data for Atlanta and Houston were gathered in 1971. Data for Chicago and San Francisco-Oakland were collected during 1973-74.

TABLE A.34

Contractors Interviewed, by Proportion of Work Performed for Anglo Customers: By City and Racial/Ethnic Background

Proportion of work performed for Anglo customers	Atlanta Black	Houston Black	Houston Spanish-American	Houston Total	Subtotal, Cities in South	Chicago Black	Chicago Spanish-American	Chicago Total
How much of your business do Anglo customers constitute?								
0 None	3	2	1	3	6	—	3	3
1 Less than 10 percent (but not 0)	4	2	2	4	8	3	2	5
2 10 to 49 percent	8	1	4	5	13	5	3	8
3 50 to 90 percent	12	3	8	11	23	10	3	13
4 More than 90 percent (but not 100)	3	1	4	5	8	7	1	8
5 100 percent	—	1	9	10	10	1	4	5
Some, but extent unspecified	11	1	17	18	29	—	—	—
Total respondents	41	11	45	56	97	26	16	42

Proportion of work performed for Anglo customers	Black American	Spanish-American	San Francisco–Oakland				Total	Subtotal, Cities in non-South	Total Minorities, All Cities
			Spaniard-American	Chinese-American	Japanese-American	American Indian			
How much of your business do Anglo customers consti-tute?									
0 None	—	1	—	—	—	—	1	4	10
1 Less than 10 percent (but not 0)	5	1	—	6	—	—	12	17	25
2 10 to 49 percent	12	4	—	5	2	—	23	31	44
3 50 to 90 percent	42	7	1	4	2	1	57	70	93
4 More than 90 percent (but not 100)	13	9	4	2	1	1	30	38	46
5 100 percent	15	2	1	—	1	—	19	24	34
Some, but extent unspecified	—	—	—	—	—	—	—	—	—
Total respondents	87	24	6	17	6	2	142	184	281

Source: Personal interviews with minority contractors. Data for Atlanta and Houston were gathered in 1971. Data for Chicago and San Francisco–Oakland were collected during 1973–74.

Mentioned Sources of Information on Jobs for Contractors Interviewed:
By City and Racial/Ethnic Background

	Formal Sources					
	Dodge Reports (or Daily Pacific Builder)	Build-er's Ex-change	Government Procurement Conferences	Govern-ment Bid Lists	Nongovern-ment Bid Lists	Other Formal Sources
Atlanta						
Black	11	1	—	2	—	8
Houston						
Black	1	—	—	—	—	3
Spanish-American	2	—	—	—	1	11
Total	3	—	—	—	1	14
Subtotal, cities in South	14	1	—	2	1	22
Chicago						
Black	11	—	—	8	1	1
Spanish-American	3	—	2	3	2	—
Total	14	—	2	11	3	1
San Francisco-Oakland						
Black	35	2	17	18	7	3
Spanish-American	5	5	—	—	—	1
Spaniard-American	6	1	1	—	2	1
Chinese-American	4	—	5	4	4	—
Japanese-American	—	—	—	—	—	—
American Indian	—	—	—	—	—	—
Total	50	8	23	22	13	5
Subtotal, cities in non-South	64	8	25	33	16	6
Total minorities, all cities	78	9	25	35	17	28
San Francisco-Oakland						
White	15	—	2	1	—	—

	Informal Sources					
	Referrals from Minority Contractors' Association	Customer Recommen-dations or Callbacks	Referrals from General Contractors or Architects	Go To Job Site and Ask	Other In-formal Sources	Total Re-spond-ents
Atlanta						
Black	5	17	7	7	12	47
Houston						
Black	5	6	3	1	2	11
Spanish-American	8	20	10	7	10	48
Total	13	26	13	8	12	59
Subtotal, cities in South	18	43	20	15	24	106
Chicago						
Black	11	14	2	3	4	24
Spanish-American	8	11	—	3	2	16
Total	19	25	2	6	6	40
San Francisco-Oakland						
Black	43	76	6	25	3	88
Spanish-American	5	16	—	2	2	24
Spaniard-American	—	8	2	2	3	8
Chinese-American	—	15	—	2	2	18
Japanese-American	—	6	—	—	—	6
American Indian	—	2	—	—	—	2
Total	48	122	8	31	10	146
Subtotal, Cities in non-South	67	147	10	37	16	186
Total Minorities, all cities	85	190	30	52	40	292
San Francisco-Oakland						
White	—	20	—	—	—	24

Note: Columns may not add to total respondents because many contractors mentioned more than one source of information on jobs.

Source: Personal interviews with construction contractors. Data for Atlanta and Houston were gathered in 1971. Data for Chicago and San Francisco-Oakland were collected during 1973-74.

TABLE A.36

Contractors Interviewed,
By Attitude toward Size of Current Work Load:
By City and Racial/Ethnic Background

	Are you currently getting all the work you can handle?			Total Respondents
	Yes	No	As a Percent of Total Respondents	
Atlanta				
Black	27	9	25	36
Houston				
Black	7	4	36	11
Spanish-American	24	19	44	43
TOTAL	31	23	43	54
SUBTOTAL,				
Cities in South	58	32	36	90
Chicago				
Black	16	10	39	26
Spanish-American	6	10	63	16
TOTAL	22	20	48	42
San Francisco-Oakland				
Black	28	61	69	89
Spanish-American	10	14	58	24
Spaniard-American	3	5	63	8
Chinese-American	7	11	61	18
Japanese-American	3	3	50	6
American Indian	1	1	50	2
TOTAL	52	95	65	147
SUBTOTAL,				
Cities in non-South	74	115	61	189
TOTAL MINORITIES,				
All Cities	132	147	53	279

Source: Personal interviews with minority contractors. Data for Atlanta and Houston were gathered in 1971. Data for Chicago and San Francisco-Oakland were collected during 1973-74.

161

TABLE A.37

Contractors Interviewed, by Knowledge of and Participation in
SBA Programs: By City and Racial/Ethnic Background

	San Francisco-Oakland	Atlanta 1971	
	White	Black	Black
8(a) program			
Not heard of it	9	30	6
Familiar with it	6	14	5
Application submitted	1	4	3
Rejected	—	—	—
Pending	—	—	—
Accepted	1	4	3
Contract(s) obtained	1	—	1
TOTAL RESPONDENTS	15	44	11
Revokable, revolving line of credit			
Not heard of it	11		
Familiar with it	5		
Application submitted	—		
Rejected	—		Not Yet
Pending	—		
Accepted	1		
TOTAL RESPONDENTS	16		
Bonding guarantee program			
Not heard of it	10		
Familiar with it	5		
Application submitted	1		
Rejected	—		Not Yet
Pending	—		
Accepted	1		
TOTAL RESPONDENTS	15		

			San
		Spanish-	Spaniard-
	Black	American	American
8(a) program			
Not heard of it	21	8	5
Familiar with it	70	17	1
Application submitted	36	6	—
Rejected	3	—	—
Pending	—	—	—
Accepted	33	6	—
Contract(s) obtained	12	5	—
TOTAL RESPONDENTS	91	25	6
Revokable, revolving line of credit			
Not heard of it	42	14	5
Familiar with it	49	10	1
Application submitted	13	3	—
Rejected	3	—	—
Pending	—	—	—
Accepted	10	3	—
TOTAL RESPONDENTS	91	24	6
Bonding guarantee program			
Not heard of it	28	14	5
Familiar with it	63	11	1
Application submitted	22	3	—
Rejected	2	—	—
Pending	1	—	—
Accepted	19	3	—
TOTAL RESPONDENTS	91	25	6

Source: Personal interviews with contractors. Data for Atlanta and Houston were gathered

162

Houston-1971 Spanish-American	Total	Subtotals, Cities in South	Chicago-1973-74 Black	Spanish-American	Total
37	43	73	5	4	9
9	14	28	21	12	33
2	5	9	11	3	14
—	—	—	—	—	—
—	—	—	1	—	1
2	5	9	10	3	13
1	2	2	6	2	8
46	57	101	26	16	42
			7	10	17
			19	6	25
			9	3	12
Implemented			2	—	2
			3	1	4
			4	2	6
			26	16	42
			11	6	17
			14	9	23
			5	3	8
Implemented			—	—	—
			—	—	—
			5	3	8
			25	15	40

Francisco-Oakland Chinese-American	Japanese-American	American Indian	Total	Subtotals, Cities in non-South	Total Minorities, All Cities
6	3	2	45	54	127
12	3	—	103	136	164
8	1	—	51	65	74
—	—	—	3	3	3
—	—	—	—	1	1
8	1	—	48	61	70
5	—	—	22	30	32
18	6	2	148	190	291
13	6	1	81	98	98
5	—	1	66	91	91
1	—	—	17	29	29
—	—	—	4	6	6
—	—	—	—	4	4
—	—	—	13	19	19
18	6	2	147	189	189
9	5	1	62	79	79
9	1	1	86	109	109
5	1	—	31	39	39
1	—	—	3	3	3
—	—	—	1	1	1
4	1	—	27	35	35
18	6	2	148	188	188

in 1971. Data for Chicago and San Francisco-Oakland were collected during 1973-74.

TABLE A.38

Minority Contractors Interviewed, by Expressed Preferences for Government
Assistance: By City and Racial/Ethnic Background

	Increasing Availability of Financing	Increasing Volume of Contracts	Area of Preference Assistance with Bonding	Technical Assistance	Labor Training	Legal Action Against Discrimination	Other	Total Respondents
Atlanta								
Black	17	3	1	5	6	—	—	21
Houston								
Black	6	1	2	2	2	1	—	8
Spanish-American	10	1	1	4	2	—	3	16
TOTAL	16	2	3	6	4	1	3	24
SUBTOTAL, Cities in South	33	5	4	11	10	1	3	45
Chicago								
Black	10	3	3	—	2	1	13	22
Spanish-American	7	12	1	2	1	4	2	15
TOTAL	17	15	4	2	3	5	15	37
San Francisco-Oakland								
Black	80	51	27	19	9	13	1	86
Spanish-American	12	10	5	5	1	2	5	22
Spaniard-American	4	—	—	—	1	—	2	7
Chinese-American	5	7	2	5	1	—	1	14
Japanese-American	—	2	—	2	1	—	1	5
American Indian	2	2	—	—	1	—	—	2
TOTAL	103	72	34	31	12	15	10	136
SUBTOTAL, Cities in non-South	120	87	38	33	15	20	25	173
TOTAL MINORITIES, All Cities	153	92	42	44	25	21	28	218

Source: Personal interviews with minority contractors. Data for Atlanta and Houston were gathered in 1971. Data for Chicago and San Francisco–Oakland were collected during 1973–74.

TABLE A.39

Contractors Interviewed, by Joint-venture Experience:
By City and Racial/Ethnic Background

	Joint-venture Experience							
	With White Firm	With Minority Firm	With Both White and Minority Firm	With Unspecified Firm	Total With Joint-venture Experience	As a Percent of Total Respondents	Total Without Joint-venture Experience	Total Respondents
Atlanta								
Black	0	9	0	0	9	20	35	44
Houston								
Black	0	3	0	0	3	30	7	10
Spanish-American	0	12	0	0	12	27	33	45
TOTAL	0	15	0	0	15	27	40	55
SUBTOTAL, Cities in South	0	24	0	0	24	24	75	99
Chicago								
Black	6	1	1	1	9	35	17	26
Spanish-American	0	3	0	0	3	19	13	16
TOTAL	6	4	1	1	12	29	30	42
San Francisco-Oakland								
Black	14	6	5	0	25	28	64	89
Spanish-American	6	0	0	0	6	25	18	24
Spaniard-American	1	0	0	0	1	12	7	8
Chinese-American	2	0	0	0	2	11	16	18
Japanese-American	0	1	0	0	1	17	5	6
American Indian	1	0	0	0	1	50	1	2
TOTAL	24	7	5	0	36	24	111	147
SUBTOTAL, Cities in non-South	30	11	6	1	48	25	141	189
TOTAL MINORITIES, All Cities	30	35	6	1	72	25	216	288
San Francisco-Oakland White	10	0	0	0	10	40	15	25

Source: Personal interviews with contractors. Data for Atlanta and Houston were gathered in 1971. Data for Chicago and San Francisco-Oakland were collected during 1973-74.

TABLE A.40

Contractors Interviewed, by Willingness to Joint-venture :
By City and Racial/Ethnic Background

	Willing to Joint-venture	As a Percent of Total Respondents	Not Willing to Joint-venture	Total Respondents
Atlanta				
Black	33	83	7	40
Houston				
Black	6	67	3	9
Spanish-American	26	60	17	43
TOTAL	32	62	20	52
SUBTOTAL, Cities in South	65	71	27	92
Chicago				
Black	24	92	2	26
Spanish-American	11	79	3	14
TOTAL	35	88	5	40
San Francisco—Oakland				
Black	73	82	16	89
Spanish-American	18	75	6	24
Spaniard-American	4	50	4	8
Chinese-American	16	89	2	18
Japanese-American	4	67	2	6
American Indian	1	50	1	2
TOTAL	116	79	31	147
SUBTOTAL, Cities in non-South	151	81	36	187
TOTAL MINORITIES, All Cities	216	77	63	279
San Francisco—Oakland White	17	68	8	25

Source: Personal interviews with contractors. Data for Atlanta and Houston were gathered in 1971. Data for Chicago and San Francisco-Oakland were collected during 1973-74.

166

TABLE A.41

Expansion Plans of Minority Contractors Interviewed:
By City and Racial/Ethnic Background

	Want to Expand	Preference Category As a Percent of Total Respondents	Do Not Want To Expand	Total Respondents
Atlanta				
Black	40	80	10	50
Houston				
Black	9	75	4	13
Spanish-American	34	69	15	49
TOTAL	43	69	19	62
SUBTOTAL, Cities in South	83	74	29	112
Chicago				
Black	21	81	5	26
Spanish-American	14	88	2	16
TOTAL	35	83	7	42
San Francisco-Oakland				
Black	62	74	22	84
Spanish-American	15	75	5	20
Spaniard-American	7	88	1	8
Chinese-American	14	78	4	18
Japanese-American	3	50	3	6
American Indian	—	—	2	2
TOTAL	101	73	37	138
SUBTOTAL, Cities in non-South	136	76	44	180
TOTAL MINORITIES, All Cities	219	75	73	292
San Francisco-Oakland				
White	15	67	9	24

Source: Personal interviews with contractors. Data for Atlanta and Houston were gathered in 1971. Data for Chicago and San Francisco-Oakland were collected during 1973-74.

TABLE A.42

Contractors Interviewed, by Knowledge of the JOBS Program:
By City and Racial/Ethnic Background

	Aware of JOBS Program	Not Aware of JOBS Program	Total Respondents
Chicago			
Black	7	17	24
Spanish–American	—	12	12
TOTAL	7	29	36
San Francisco–Oakland			
Black	34	50	84
Spanish–American	4	18	22
Spaniard–American	1	6	7
Chinese–American	2	16	18
Japanese–American	—	4	4
American Indian	1	1	2
TOTAL	42	95	137
TOTAL MINORITIES,			
Both Cities	49	124	173
San Francisco–Oakland			
White	9	9	18

Source: Personal interviews with contractors during 1973–74. Similar data were not collected in Atlanta and Houston.

168

TABLE A.43

Contractors Interviewed, by Participation in Formal Training Programs: By City and Racial/Ethnic Background

| | | | Has Your Firm Participated in Any Formal Training Program During the Past Five Years? | | | | | | |
| | | | Type of Program | | | | | | Total Respondents |
	No	Yes	Apprenticeship	NAB–JOBS	Other Governmental	Other Private	Both Governmental and Private	Unspecified	
Atlanta									
Black	29	9	4	2	2	1	—	—	38
Houston									
Black	7	4	—	—	3	1	—	—	11
Spanish-American	42	3	2	—	1	—	—	—	45
TOTAL	49	7	2	—	4	1	—	—	56
SUBTOTAL, Cities in South	78	16	6	2	6	2	—	—	94
Chicago									
Black	15	11	6	—	—	5	—	—	26
Spanish-American	11	3	2	—	—	1	—	—	14
TOTAL	26	14	8	—	—	6	—	—	40
San Francisco–Oakland									
Black	50	39	3	1	19	9	5	2	89
Spanish-American	17	6	1	—	1	3	1	—	23
Spaniard-American	6	2	2	—	1	—	—	—	8
Chinese-American	11	7	1	—	5	1	—	—	18
Japanese-American	4	2	—	—	—	2	—	—	6
American Indian	—	2	—	—	1	1	—	—	2
TOTAL	88	58	7	1	26	16	6	2	146
SUBTOTAL, Cities in non-South	114	72	15	1	26	22	6	2	186
TOTAL MINORITIES, All Cities	192	88	21	3	32	24	6	2	280
San Francisco–Oakland									
White	9	15	—	—	3	4	2	—	24

Source: Personal interviews with contractors. Data for Atlanta and Houston were gathered in 1971. Data for Chicago and San Francisco–Oakland were collected during 1973–74.

169

"Aid for Minorities." Engineering News-Record, December 11, 1969, p. 68.

Allgood, William T., and Francis S. Ridgeway. "Sweating Out Business Loans." Manpower 3 (July 1971): 23-27.

Associated General Contractors of American, Education and Research Foundation. Construction Education Directory. 2d. ed. Washington, D.C., 1974.

Bates, Timothy. "Employment Potential of Inner City Black Enterprise." The Review of Black Political Economy 4 (Summer 1974): 59-67.

"Black Builders' Aid." Engineering News-Record, September 11, 1969, p. 52.

"Black Contractors Sharpen Their Pencils." Engineering News-Record, July 3, 1969, p. 48.

"Black Contractor Turns Off Black Pickets." Engineering News-Record, April 30, 1970, p. 52.

"Building Up Minority Contractors." Manpower 1 (October 1969): 23-25.

Campbell, James R. "Cleveland Operations' Equal Opportunity Program." Cleveland, Ohio: Turner Construction Company, 1970.

Case, Frederick E. Black Capitalism: Problems in Development, A Case Study of Los Angeles. New York: Praeger, 1972.

Coles, Flournoy A., Jr. "Unique Problems of Black Businessmen." The Review of Black Political Economy 5 (Fall 1974): 45-56.

Debro, Joseph. "The Minority Builder." Labor Law Journal 25 (May 1970): 290-309.

_____. "Financing Minority Contractors." Bankers Magazine 154 (Winter 1971): 70-76.

Delaney, Paul. "Blacks Eye Militancy for Building Jobs." New York Times, June 27, 1971.

Dublinsky, Irwin. "Trade Union Discrimination in the Pittsburgh Construction Industry: How and Why it Operates." Urban Affairs Quarterly 6 (March 1971): 297-318.

_____. Reform in Trade Union Discrimination in the Construction Industry. New York: Praeger, 1973.

Dunlop, John T., and D. Quinn Mills. "Manpower in Construction: A Profile of the Industry and Projections to 1975." In Report of the President's Committee on Urban Housing. Vol. 2, Technical Studies, Washington, D.C.: Government Printing Office, 1968, pp. 241-86.

"For Minority Contractors . . . A Fair Share." Constructor 54
     (September 1972): 12-15.
"Ford Boosts Aid to Minority Builders." Engineering News-Record,
     April 10, 1969, p. 147.
Ford Foundation, National Affairs Division. Minority Contractor
     Bonding Program: A Manual of Organizational Steps and Pro-
     cedures. New York, 1968.
"Fred Eversley Aims for the Top." Engineering News-Record,
     July 31, 1969, pp. 27, 28, 31.
"Grant Promotes Minority Builders." Engineering News-Record,
     July 11, 1968, pp. 27-29.
"Grants Boost Minority Workers Training." Engineering News-
     Record, December 5, 1968, p. 55.
"GSA Prescribes Rules for Minority Contracting." Engineering
     News Record, September 23, 1971, p. 45.
Hain, Edward B., Jr. "Black Workers versus White Unions: Alter-
     native Strategies in the Construction Industry." Wayne Law
     Review 16 (Winter 1969): 37-76.
"Homebuilder Seeks Out Minority Contractors." Engineering News-
     Record, April 9, 1969, p. 154.
"HUD, OMBE, and SBA Project to Employ Minority Contractors in
     Home Repair." Fair Employment Report, July 1, 1974, p. 12.
"HUD to Get Contractor List." Engineering News-Record, July 10,
     1969, p. 84.
"HUD Seeks More Minority Jobs." Engineering News-Record,
     September 18, 1969, p. 246.
Immel, A. Richard. "How a 'Breakthrough' in Black-Run Business
     Collapsed in Costly Ruin." Wall Street Journal, August 23,
     1972.
Jones, Jack. "Fund Plan Called Breakthrough for Minority Con-
     tractor Groups." Los Angeles Times, August 6, 1970.
_____. "Money for Minority Contractors Lagging." Los Angeles
     Times, February 22, 1971.
Juarez and Associates. A Report: National Survey of Minority
     Professionals and Businesses in Housing Production and
     Urban Development. Los Angeles, 1972.
Mills, Daniel Quinn. Industrial Relations and Manpower in Con-
     struction. Cambridge, Mass.: MIT Press, 1972.
"Minorities Grow More Militant as Chicago Antibias Plan Fails."
     Engineering News-Record, July 8, 1971, p. 48.
Minority Builder Magazine. Various issues.
"Minority Contractors Form New Group." Engineering News-
     Record, August 14, 1969, p. 61.
"Minority Contractors Get Help." Engineering News-Record,
     December 18, 1969, p. 173.

"Minority Contractors Get Some of the Action." Engineering News-Record, March 12, 1970, p. 55.

"Minority Contractors Reassured Government Supports Their Efforts." Engineering News-Record, July 1, 1971, p. 12.

Mitchell, Howard E., Marion B. Fox, and James S. Roberts. "A Report to President Gaylord P. Harnwell on the University of Pennsylvania Employment Policy in the Construction Trades." Mimeographed. Philadelphia: Human Resources Center, University of Pennsylvania, 1969.

"Negro Contractors Form a Corporation." Engineering News-Record, January 16, 1969, p. 58.

"New Doors Open for Minority Contractors." Black Enterprise (February 1974): 21-23.

Patterson, Pat. "Construction Opportunity on the Rise." Black Enterprise 1 (March 1971): 16-21, 44.

Poinsett, Alex. "From Plasterer to Plutocrat: Herman J. Russell Shows How 'the System Can Be Had.'" Ebony, May 1973, pp. 85-87, 90, 94, 96.

"Project Will Extend Aid to Minority Contractors." New Orleans Times Picayune, July 21, 1971.

Pugh, G. Douglas. "Bonding Minority Contractors." In Black Economic Development, edited by William F. Haddad and G. Douglas Pugh, pp. 138-50. Englewood Cliffs, N.J.: Prentice-Hall, 1969.

"The SBA Bond Guarantee." Black Enterprise, February 1972, p. 54.

"SBA Lends a Hand to Minority Contractors." Engineering News-Record, January 15, 1970, pp. 14-15.

"SBA Program of Subcontracting under Widespread Legal Attack." Engineering News-Record, January 27, 1972, p. 15.

Schorr, Burt. "Black Construction Contractors Find Selves Cut Out of Lucrative Long-Term Contracts." Wall Street Journal, May 7, 1971.

Shapiro, Theresa R. "Black Builders in Greater New Orleans." Louisiana Business Survey 2 (July 1971): 10-12.

Shimberg, Benjamin, Barbara F. Esser, and Daniel H. Kruger. Occupational Licensing: Practices and Policies. Washington, D.C.: Public Affairs Press, 1972.

Stone, Michael. "Project Equality Today: A Case Study of the Church in the Social Order." The Christian Century, January 21, 1970, pp. 79-82.

Stuart, Reginald. Black Contractors' Dilemma. Nashville, Tenn.: Race Relations Information Center. 1971.

_____. "Construction Lag Hurts Minority Builders." New York Times, June 17, 1974.

"A Successful Black Contractor's Advice on How to Succeed: Get
    Big." Engineering News-Record, September 9, 1971, pp.
    18-19.

"2.89 Million Pledged to Launch MCAP." OMBE Outlook, August
    1970.

"The United Builders Association of Chicago." Chicago: United
    Builders Association of Chicago, 1971.

U.S. Bureau of the Census. Minority-Owned Businesses: 1969.
    Report MB-1. Washington, D.C.: Government Printing
    Office, 1971.

U.S. Commission on Civil Rights. The Federal Civil Rights En-
    forcement Effort. Washington, D.C.: Government Printing
    Office, 1971.

U.S. Department of Commerce, Office of Minority Business Enter-
    prise. Special Catalogue of Federal Programs Assisting
    Minority Enterprise. Washington, D.C.: Government Printing
    Office, 1971.

U.S. Department of Housing and Urban Development, Office of the
    Assistant Secretary for Equal Opportunity. Minority Business
    Opportunities. Washington, D.C.: Government Printing Office,
    1970.

_____. Registry of Minority Construction Contractors, vols. 1-6.
    Washington, D.C.: Government Printing Office, 1970.

_____. A Survey of Minority Construction Contractors. Washing-
    ton, D.C.: Government Printing Office, 1971.

_____. Registry of Minority Contractors and Housing Professionals,
    vols. 1-10. Washington, D.C.: Government Printing Office, 1973.

U.S. Small Business Administration, Reports Management Division.
    Firms Approved for 8(a) Contract Assistance. Washington,
    D.C., December 1972.

"Urban Coalition Unveils Plan to Bolster Minority Contractors."
    Manpower Information Service 1 (July 29, 1970): 9.

Venable, Abraham S. "Black Business Development: Chaos in
    Transition? (Part 4)." Black Enterprise, December 1971,
    pp. 48, 50, 52.

_____. Building Black Business: An Analysis and a Plan. New
    York: Earl G. Graves, 1972.

ABOUT THE AUTHOR AND
ABOUT THE CENTER
FOR THE STUDY OF HUMAN RESOURCES

ROBERT W. GLOVER is Acting Director of the Center for the Study of Human Resources, the University of Texas at Austin.

In addition to his work on minority enterprise, Dr. Glover has written several articles and reports on equal employment opportunity and apprenticeship. One of his recent monographs, written with William S. Franklin and Ray Marshall, was <u>Training and Entry into Union Construction</u>.

Dr. Glover received a B.A. from the University of Santa Clara and an M.A. and Ph.D. from the University of Texas at Austin.

Initiated in June, 1970 by Ray Marshall, the Center for the Study of Human Resources, the University of Texas at Austin, is an interdisciplinary research and training center focused on policy issues concerning education and training, labor markets, equal opportunity, and rural development. Whenever possible, research projects are linked to demonstration efforts to field-test ideas in operating projects.

Key attention is devoted to the following subjects related to human resource development:

1. economic policy, particularly economic development of lagging regions and unemployed, underemployed, or subemployed people;

2. manpower programs, which include labor market adjustment procedures, job information and projections, the movement of workers between areas, skill training, pre-employment training, and public employment;

3. antidiscrimination programs and policies;

4. education, with special emphasis on the role of education in the preparation for work; and

5. health, welfare, and income maintenance, with special emphasis on the use of these activities to support manpower programs.

HOUSING FINANCE AGENCIES: A Comparison between State
Agencies and HUD
Nathan S. Betnun

MINORITY ACCESS TO FEDERAL GRANTS-IN-AID: The Gap
Between Policy and Performance
John Hope, II

MINORITIES IN U.S. INSTITUTIONS OF HIGHER EDUCATION
Frank Brown
Madelon D. Stent

A SURVEY OF CHINESE-AMERICAN MANPOWER AND
EMPLOYMENT
Betty Lee Sung